CHINESE BOXING

CHINESE BOXING

Masters and Methods

Robert W. Smith

North Atlantic Books
Berkeley, California

Published by North Atlantic Books
P.O. Box 12327
Berkeley, California 94712

Printed in the United States of America

Chinese Boxing: Masters and Methods is sponsored by the Society for the Study of Native Arts and Sciences, a nonprofit educational corporation whose goals are to develop an educational and cross-cultural perspective linking various scientific, social, and artistic fields; to nurture a holistic view of arts, sciences, humanities, and healing; and to publish and distribute literature on the relationship of mind, body, and nature.

ISBN 1-55643-095-7 (cloth)
ISBN 1-55643-085-X (pbk.)

5   6   7   8   9   10   /   04   03   02   01   00

Contents

ACKNOWLEDGMENTS

I nod appreciatively to those Western martial arts colleagues who read the manuscript and suggested changes or who aided in other ways: Warren Conner, Ben Fusaro, Tam Gibbs, Evy Jordan, Tony Levelle, Gordon Martin, Bill Mason, Ivan Maygutiak, Ralph Strauch, Dale Ward, Jerry Watt, Art Wohl, and Andy Zaleta. And I bow from the waist to all my Chinese friends who helped directly and indirectly with the book. They are its substance and are identified in it. And finally, I kowtow to my girl friend Alice and to Doris Leufroy, who after typing through a maze of Chinese names and terms still came up sunshiny smiling.

Introduction

A decade ago I lived in Taiwan and traveled throughout Southeast Asia, where, in my off-duty hours, I pursued the study of Chinese
boxing (*ch'uan shu*). I sweated and researched. I came back loaded
with 16 mm motion picture film, thousands of photographs, reams
of translations, hundreds of books, and several volumes of notes
made during daily practice. To reduce this mass to easy compre-
hension has taken almost a decade and has resulted in several books.[1]
The present work attempts to throw light on the men and methods
I encountered. In no sense metaphysical, it is a pragmatic account
of how an outsider set about learning an art that combines the
hardness of a wall and the softness of a butterfly's wings.

No national form of fighting approaches Chinese boxing in the
diversity and profundity of its forms. Traditionally, Chinese boxing
has been either taught by verbal instruction, without books, or
caught by secrets handed down by teachers to trusted students.
Although effective as a means of transmitting a worthwhile system,
this method was vulnerable to amateurs' stealing and modifying
part of the corpus. My intention has been to reflect the real, so that
the reader may be equipped to reject the chicanery of the charlatans
and their associates in the media. What passes in the West as *kung fu*
(even the name is a distortion) is ludicrous by comparison.[2]

Perhaps what I write will help to offset the silly, sensational way
in which Chinese boxing is reflected in the media, particularly in
"*kung-fu*" movies—a good name for them, incidentally, since the term
kung fu is an American bastardization that is meant to mean but does
not mean boxing. Based on woefully inadequate knowledge, these
films invariably distort facts. The fighting is the product of combining fake karate (a no-contact regime) with cameras, trampolines,

and inspired sound effects. The effect is camp of the lowest order, so bad in fact that it is laughable. This aspect has led reviewers to acquiesce in this rubbish: after all, if it is laughable who can be hurt? They are unaware—nor do producers care—that many young people watch, believe, and imitate this nonsense.

Bertolt Brecht, in his poem "Legendary Origin of the Book Tao-te-Ching During Lao-tse's Journey Into Exile," tells the old familiar story. Going westward into exile, Lao-tse is stopped by a customs guard. When the guard learns that the old philosopher is leaving society, he implores him to stop a while and put pen to his thoughts. Lao-tse agrees:

> Snubbing of politely put suggestions
> Seems to be unheard of by the old.
> For the old man said: "Those who ask questions
> Earn straight answers. . . ."

We are thankful for Lao-tse and his world-wringing thoughts.

> And we've this to thank the guard about:
> He was there to draw it out.

In learning traditional Chinese boxing, I looked on myself as a catalyst eliciting information on a little-known aspect of Chinese culture, overgrown and obscured by legend.

The unscientific approach most Chinese take to boxing encumbered my work in this vineyard. They believe that boxers can do outlandishly incredible things, for the performance of which the laws of physics are suspended. Much of this fancy I was able to prune. But some remains. Why? Simply because some of it is more than possible, and I now keep an open mind on it. Some of the rest I saw and experienced and have no scientific means to challenge. On the subject of ch'i, however, I have no open mind. I am as biased on it as a scream from the dentist's chair. I believe it exists. The only reason one has for doubting it is that he has never experienced it.

Therefore, my toleration of those who disbelieve is tinged with the hearty encouragement that they have a readiness to let themselves be seized by it. I have no doubt that studies of bio-feedback and allied efforts probing the mind-body relationship will in the not too distant future prove the truth of my contention.

Practice varied with the instructor. In general, it was not as rigorous as that in a Japanese karate *dōjō*. But the more sophisticated movements I learned more than outweighed the difference in exertion levels. This rationale broke down, however, in Chinese commercial gyms, where, more often than not, no rigor was imposed even in learning elementary boxing postures. I tested such gyms early and found the teachers inferior and the substance wanting. It was difficult to break a sweat and, because of the tea and conversation interruptions, difficult to maintain it. My approach is embraced in Jung's line: "Consciousness is not achieved without pain." Thus, even with a master espousing an exemplary system, it is necessary to throw oneself fully into the teaching. Particularly is this true when one has not been blessed with innate talent, and I candidly felt that I had not been so lucky.

The discipline I set for myself was taxing. No one teacher, no one system could have tired me so. Even the hardest Shao-lin methods stopped short of full exhaustion, based on the belief that every technique is inseparable from its psychic context; thus, the over-worked body can take punishment resiliently, but the mind needs time to assimilate and embrace the total teaching. But I had only three years—all too short a time. So I had to make the hours do for me what the too few years could not. The upshot was that I studied from several teachers concurrently. I spent hours every day of the week learning and other hours thinking through and digesting what I had learned. Fatigue became my constant companion and I learned to live with bone aches, pulled muscles, bone chips, and utter exhaustion. Pain became for me only an opinion, one I chose not to have. The closest thing in literature expressing my state is the poem by John Heywood (ca. 1497–ca. 1580), "Jack and His Father."

"Jack," quoth his father, "how shall I ease take?
If I stand, my legs ache, and if I kneel
My knees ache; If I go, then my feet ache;
If I lie, my back aches; if I sit, I feel
My hips ache; and lean I never so well,
My elbows ache." "Sir," quoth Jack, "pain in exile,
Since all these ease not, best ye hang awhile."

The task was made easier by the knowledge that it was self-
imposed; I could break off at any time I chose. But a bigger factor in
it was desire. And so, believing with Confucius that "to review and
practice what one has studied, day after day, that also is a joy," I
plunged into a three-year swim. And though I fell asleep often in my
Chinese class, and my wife began to call me "Brother Bob," I made
peace with exhaustion and tempted learning from the teaching.

The historian J. H. Plumb, and many others in the West, feel
that the British pioneered the view that games form character. True,
in the West, Britain was preeminent in this endeavor, but many
years earlier the Chinese had placed character as the summum
bonum of athletic endeavor. Until the Warring States period (403–
221 B.C.) even warfare was conducted as a game; rank was deferred
to in battle, arrows were released in turn, and grain was sent to
besieged enemies. Later, as boxing developed and was stimulated by
Buddhist and Taoist sources, it stressed self-development, not only
in point of technique but, more importantly, as regards the inner
quality of its adherents. It has continued so to the present, at a time
when we in the West have become cynical about the notion that
character is a derivative of athletics. Commercialization has almost
killed it for us: we look to the crowd and forget the player.

I say *almost* advisedly, because I believe that an exercise, a game, a
book, a poem, or a symphony can still impact on a waiting heart.
Albert Camus once said that the only lessons in moral ethics he ever
learned came from playing soccer at the University of Algiers. A
discipline can test and mold a man, and the present difficulties in the

world may fairly be attributed to the fact that men in power have no discipline: they play roles instead of games. But a discipline that becomes masochistic is perhaps worse than none. Camus mused in another place: "Four months of ascetic, solitary life. The will, the mind gain from it. But the heart?" The Indiana poet Max Ehrmann, in "Desiderata," put it this way: "Beyond a wholesome discipline, be gentle with yourself."

In a work of this kind there is always the danger of what Mark Twain called "creative memory," the remembering of things that are not so. I have attempted to purge this kind of memory ruthlessly. But because so many readers have criticized me for my past terseness, I have dilated here at times so that the reader can savor the flavor of these men and their methods. In this way the reader may cross the spatial and temporal barriers and share the experience with me. I have avoided the rash of foot-and-note disease and have tried to see things steadily and whole and to explain them clearly.

I met some great boxers and many frauds. Many who posed as experts could not meet Carl Sandburg's definition: "An expert is any man who can spit over a boxcar." The frauds, unfortunately, are the ones most accessible to foreigners. The good ones lie back, wait and watch. This means that one must be blessed with friends, manners, money, patience, and luck if he is to avoid the quacks and get tuition from the real masters. I was so blessed. Moreover, the more I read from the mainland, the more I feel that by studying under the cream of the boxer crop that came out to Taiwan, I studied under the best. The mainland government has put everyone, including boxers, to work, and the territory there may now be barren.

This is only a small catalogue of Chinese boxers and their methods. There were many others who came across my vision and as quickly vanished without their names being recorded. And there were some who requested anonymity. "I would not have you monks of whom there are plenty, but men of whom there are few" goes the old Buddhist line. Besides being teachers and friends, these were men in the highest sense (figure 1).

1. *Chinese Boxing Association in Taiwan, 1960*
1. *Li Mou-ch'ing* 2. *Wu Han-chung* 3. *Fu Chia-p'in* 4. *P'an Wen-tou* 5. *Peter Chen* 6. *Liang Tung-tsai* 7. *Han Ch'ing-t'ang* 8. *Shen Mou-hui* 9. *T'ang K'o-shu* 10. *Li Tao-k'uei* 11. *Weng Ju-yuan* 12. *Chou Chi-ch'un* 13. *Wang Tzu-sheng* 14. *Wang Tzu-ho* 15. *Lu Tsung-jen* 16. *Kung chen-yu* 17. *Chen T'ien-i* 18. *Ku Chung-nien* 19. *Chang Hsiang-san* 20. *Huang Sheng-fa* 21. *Chiang Ch'ang-ken* 22. *Liao Wan-pao* 23. *Li I-ch'un* 24. *Ch'iao Ch'ang-hung* 25. *Ch'i Mei-chuan* 26. *Li Tsung-huang* 27. *Ch'en Chao-ying* 28. *Wang Ch'eng-chang* 29. *Ch'en P'an-ling* 30. *Ch'iu Pin-Ts'un* 31. *Liu Mu-sen* 32. *Yuan Tao* 33. *Liao Wu-ch'ang* 34. *Yuan T'ien-pao*

1. The Not=so=little Elephant

To be lucky in the beginning is everything.
CERVANTES

THE FIRST THING is to find a teacher. Now there are teachers and teachers. I did not agree with Krishnamurti's thought that the very institution of teacher is a fraud, but I did think that a teacher should provide more than the rudiments of a skill.[1] I believe with Kimon Nicholaides that "The job of the teacher . . . is . . . to teach students how to learn. They must acquire some real method of finding out facts for themselves lest they be limited for the rest of their lives to the facts the instructor relates . . ." I was fortunate in this from the start: my first teachers, Hung I-hsiang and Liao Wu-ch'ang, neither of whom was formally educated, exemplified this approach. This is how it was.

On arriving in Taipei in August, 1959, I immediately began practicing judo with Anderson Lin (fourth-grade black belt), Taiwan champion in 1958 and runner-up in 1959 and 1960. Lin was an amiable gent, in love with judo, and we had some great skirmishes. When I told him that I planned to do little judo during my tour—instead, I wanted to learn Chinese boxing—he was surprised. He knew little of Chinese boxing, he said, but remembered as a boy seeing a medicine hawker slice a brick like a cake as he gave his low-voiced spiel. But he did know Hung I-hsiang, a "hard" boxer. He took me to him.

My first meeting with Hung left me disappointed. He looked the epitome of an athlete gone to pot: overweight, unshaven, with an omnipresent cigarette dangling from his lips. Coming from the judo tradition, of sober ritual and cleanliness, it was something of a shock. Despite a background that included southern Shao‑lin, judo, Okinawan *gyakute*, T'ai‑chi, northern Shao‑lin, Hsing‑i, Pa‑kua, and Ch'i‑kung, the first impression took a while to correct—almost a year in fact. I was a member of a small class of foreigners being taught by him in a public gym. Because of his tremendous power, I persevered for a year. But finally I tired of the endless forms, which were largely dances (the danger that Gichin Funakoshi, the father of Japanese karate, warned against)—because they were left unex‑ plained—the ever‑present tea, and the many sessions in which the class did not break a sweat. Discipline was what was lacking. Struthers Burt, the poet, once said: "The human soul cannot function without some sort of discipline any more than water can function without pipes to impound it, and, on the other hand, the human soul cannot function if these pipes are clogged by the refuse of antiquity." My time I deemed too valuable and Chinese boxing too fertile to mark time. I pulled away.

He then sought me out, wondering why I had discontinued. I told him. He nodded; he acknowledged that the teaching was geared for Americans (make it easy) but inhibited by secrecy (do not tell them too much). He suggested that we start fresh on a private basis and promised that there would be no secrets. And, with a flourish, there would be no charge. I accepted, and we met three times a week for the remainder of my stay.

I have said he was powerful. For his bulk (five feet, seven inches; 220 pounds), he moved quickly, however. He had never trained his hands or feet with a *makiwara* (a hitting post) in the karate fashion, but could break a stand of four bricks supported or two weathered bricks flush on a table with no support (figure 2). (He had broken three bricks in this way but he was not consistent; he failed the time he tried before me.) But he was quick to add that this breaking revealed nothing but static power. The *makiwara*, he said, was unnecessary; ch'i and correct technique always incorporating a circle were all that were necessary.[2]

2. *Hung I-hsiang breaking two unsup-ported bricks*

The Asian fetish for wood, brick, tile, and ice breaking is suspect. On the mainland those who did it were called "village boxers." The materials almost invariably are prepared in various ways to facilitate the breaking (this much can be said for Hung: he used only weath-ered, unprepared materials). Once at a public display, one of Hung's Chinese students broke two bricks and ostentatiously invited me to break one. I tried, but the brick obdurately remained intact. I picked it up and just as ostentatiously invited the student to break it, telling him that I had weakened it for him. He tried to refuse, but Hung got into the spirit of the thing, and the student had to try. He failed amid general merriment. The crowd that had enjoyed the foreigner's failure laughed just as hard at the failure of one of their own when faced with a trick brick. For that is what it was: a brick baked with reinforcing rods in it.

We took apart the five basic forms of Hsing-i (one of the three internal boxing methods), which he had learned from Chang Chun-feng. After practicing that of Yuan Tao, Wang Shu-chin, and Paul Kuo later, Hung's method appeared stronger but slower (thus, in the context of the internal system, inferior). He said that practicing the first step (*p'i ch'uan*, "splitting") and holding it for three breaths an hour a day would cause the ch'i to concentrate in one's fingers. I found it to be so. We then took the five forms and merged them in the "Uniting" form.

Besides Hsing-i I learned from Hung such forms as Kiangsi Five

Tiger, Eight Part Shao-lin, Roc Braces Wings, Little Nine Heaven, and one that focused on the opponent's groin, which I never learned the name for but nicknamed "Bowling Ball Kata." We also worked on formal joint methods including a Shao-lin hard form of sticking hands similar to T'ai-chi's pushing hands and did considerable unrehearsed close fighting. We pulled our punches; otherwise I would not have continued long. This was done by breaking the power at the wrist and slapping with the fist, which still could shake a person. I found him fairly slow and relatively easy to score on. Others who watched the proceedings corroborated my feeling. The key element, however, was missing. Power. He had enormous power in a static position, and when this was complemented by his body weight in motion, one could see and feel that his credentials as a fighter were bona fide.

Even with his weighty credentials, Hung continually looked for new teachers. When a highly publicized teacher of jujutsu came from Japan to give an exhibition, Hung paid fifty dollars (U.S.) for his book. The teacher came to grief in the pragmatic Chinese envi-ronment. Sponsored by the judo organization in Taiwan, Ryūhō Okuyama, founder of the Hakko school of Goshin-jutsu, was advertised in the newspapers as a man who would show that Chinese boxing lacked content (the chief culprit probably was journalistic license rather than Okuyama). Naturally, Chinese boxers flooded the exhibition. He first asked for a volunteer to encircle his expert daughter from behind. There were several quick fist fights to determine who the volunteer would be. A healthy though somewhat marked specimen finally made it up to the stage. Okuyama said that his daughter using his soft method would extri-cate herself easily from the grasp of the young bear. He encircled her and brought pressure. The more she relaxed the greater the pressure became. Finally it became evident that she had no way out. But still the grinning Chinese persisted, relenting only when she began to faint. This was a signal for several boxers to storm the stage and challenge the master. By this time Okuyama had become cognizant that he had been caught in a Chinese boxing versus judo showdown. He refused the challenges and publicly stated that he had come to Taiwan to learn from—not to challenge—Chinese boxing. The exhibition, originally scheduled for three days, was shortened to two days and the Japanese troupe left wiser. Hung was terribly upset that he had invested money before seeing Okuyama perform. The advertisement had detracted from the performance.

Periodically in our sessions, Hung would tell me of a mystery teacher under whom he was studying. Occasionally he would describe the master's teaching, all of which sounded—in Chou Ch'i⁄ch'un's (see page 84) favorite word to describe the greats of Chinese boxing—marvelous. The man taught a method of frontal *ukemi* ("falling") far superior to the standard judo side and rear *ukemi*; his *ch'in⁄na* ("seizing") was ethereal; and his *tien⁄hsueh* ("attacking vital points") was vastly superior to anything Hung had ever experienced. Naturally, I tried to talk Hung into introduc⁄ing me. He stalled insufferably. I did not even learn the master's name for two years, until one night when Hung in his cups inad⁄vertantly let it slip. The mystery man's surname was K'un, and he lived at a temple at Pai⁄sha⁄t'un near Taichung. I scoffed that this sounded like the legendary boxing figures from the bookstalls. This had the desired effect. Really, he said, K'un existed. He was well past seventy, and could sometimes be seen traveling in the entourage of Ch'en P'an⁄ling, the chairman of the Chinese Boxing Association. (See figure 1.) This rang a bell. Over time I had been able to identify all of Ch'en's associates save one, a small, erect oldster. My sources simply could not tell me anything about him except that he was from Taichung. I queried General Yang, a close friend of Ch'en, about him later. I had heard that this man was a master. Who was he? Yang's eyes widened, and his hesitation was fatal to his case. No, he said, he did not know such a man. But then, after another critical lapse, who had told me of him? I protected Hung and merely told him that I heard about him from some boxers in Taipei. That is the story. Hung was no schoolboy; he was a hardened, earthy boxer. Saki's "romance at short notice was her speciality" simply was not his forte. I am convinced that Master K'un was real and that his teaching was marvelous and only regret that I was unable to partake of it except secondhand, through Hung.

Hung was no great historical source, and some of his ideas were curious, but he was an unalloyed fighter. His reputation among boxers was high, secured through many street battles from which he had emerged unscathed. And these fights were rough affairs, swords often being employed. At least two young boxers I knew and practiced with died in such fights. But Hung survived, and grandly. He was so formidable that he often was asked to referee these battles.

Hung loved fighting, and, like Dempsey in his skirmish with the writer Paul Gallico, he was hard put to pull his punches. He once knocked me senseless with a chop to the base of the skull and often shook my entire frame with "broken power" punches. Those nights he reeked of wine were the worst, for the euphoria coupled with the lowered distance appreciation boded no good for the student. My right shoulder inherited a chronic bursitis and occasionally still remembers the hundreds of punches he demonstrated there because: (1) it was good for me to feel the power, and (2) it was the part supposedly most impervious to injury.

Even with the power, however, he was firmly wedded to the internal system. Shao-lin simply did not have the subtlety or sophistication to compare with it. I asked him once about eighty-year-old Fan Shao-ching, a Chinese living in Yokohama who was reputed to be able to pound nails into boards with his head. Hung knew him and spat with disgust. "That's all he can do, and even that is a trick—he first starts the nails with a palm-base blow."

The mind and ch'i were more important than the body, Hung said. His internal teacher had been Chang Chun-feng, then sixty-two and chief instructor at the Ministry of National Defense (figure 3). Chang's fortes were Hsing-i and Pa-kua. A storekeeper in Tientsin, he came to Taiwan in 1948 and taught many Taiwanese,

③

3. Hung's teacher, Chang Chun-feng

among them Hung I-hsiang and his brother Hung Hsien-mien. After more than a year of my badgering, Hung finally took me to Chang early one afternoon. Chang's house was modest, with five children punctuating the empty spaces. Gone in the kidneys, Chang was severe and humorless. However, his exposition of Pa-kua was first-rate, and he responded fully to my questions. He gave the linear method an authority it had in no other hands. We spent three hours talking; the time galloped as it always does when something of value is occurring.

Chang was a mixed blessing, I reflected: his book traces Hsing-i to Ta Mo and is otherwise unreliable; he himself claims to have been taught by Li Ts'un-i, Kao I-sheng, and Chang Chao-tung, but his style is harsher and rougher edged than the orthodox method taught by these masters, which makes his claim suspect. He was irascible and laconic. A mainlander, he taught Taiwanese, which reveals something about his feelings for his mainlander colleagues. And everyone he taught, he treated meanly. He was not like that great teacher of painting in Paris who was never known to have done anything except pass behind his students' easels and mutter, "Continuez, continuez." Not at all: Chang was a hard taskmaster and was quick to cuff a student around a bit to gain and keep his attention. These considerations meant nothing after I had seen his technique. I asked Hung to get me instruction from Chang. Some strange things occurred then. Initially he said that Chang refused to take me on. I persisted without success. From another direction

I started Pa-kua with another of Chang's senior students, a lean man with a large open ulcer on the side of his neck (he said it was benign). After a month he failed to appear, and I heard that the Hung brothers had scared him off, and that, in fact, Chang himself had wanted to teach me for some time but that the Hungs had told him that I was their student.

I began Pa-kua with Hung Hsien-mien shortly afterward. Fast, cocky, densely packed with pugnacity, and a heavy drinker, he was Chang's senior student in this art and conducted the master's classes for him when he was indisposed. Reportedly, he had once bested ten men in the street. And it was in the street I first met him. After whirling dervishlike through a few tactics, he invited me to hit him in the belly. He was slightly tipsy and I begged off. He insisted, I relented. It may have been the drink: struck, he sobered noticeably and looked as if he wanted to throw up. With an effort he contained himself and postponed the rest of the demonstration. Next day he passed word that he would teach me Pa-kua. In the next two years, we got through over one hundred linear forms.

Hung Hsien-mien did not last the distance, however. He begged off about halfway, pleading illness (Hung I-hsiang told me that it really was because his brother's wife wanted him to commercialize on me, which his brother refused to do), and to complete the series Hung I-hsiang shifted somewhat from teaching me seizing (ch'in-na) to Pa-kua. Although he did not have the grace of his brother in circling, he was even more authoritative in the linear forms.[3]

While concentrating on Pa-kua we continued on other aspects of boxing. I learned several intricate links of ch'in-na (one of which was to attack only the little finger offensively or defensively) and Hung's ideas on kicking. He laughed at the high kicks of karate. They were, he said, a good show but useless in a fight. When he kicked, it never went above the navel, the knee was kept straight and 220 pounds went crushingly to the target. He believed in raising the supporting foot and letting it drop or stepping forward and kicking with the rear foot; this really adds authority to the kick (figures 4–6).

4-6. Hung using a low-focused kick that follows through high

His toes were like spikes, and he kicked as well with them as with the ball of his foot. Although his fist could shatter two-inch thick planks, his best weapons were his shoulder and his top-wrist, both of which he wielded with authority. The top-wrist he directed under the arms, at the solar plexus, and at two points on the chest.

This brings us to the final stage in his teaching, attacking vital points (*tien hsueh*). He knew well the location of the vital points and deprecated karate because its method of attacking vital points (*atemi*) was so inadequate. He said that the Chinese gave the Japanese only rudiments fit for a child: karate's stance is too deep for turning, it has no short attack, the arms are held too high, it uses too much shoulder and not enough waist and does not coordinate arms and legs. He served up to me varying intensities of pain to illustrate his knowledge of my body. Although he used this ability seldom, one of his students nearly died from one of his "touches" during my stay. A stage trick of his was to stroke one's armpit, sending an electric shock through one's entire body. An even better method that I did not see was his leg touch, which reportedly left the recipient with a leg paralyzed until remedial massage permitted the unlucky one to walk again. He offered several times to do this to me, and each time I evaded with a "next time."

But on this subject he resisted showing me all. (This in spite of his telling me about a year after I started that the word had come down from on high that Smith was learning too much and that all my teachers had been admonished to go slow. He told the messenger to go to hell, and, after telling me, he said he would withhold nothing.) He had the spots from the mysterious Master K'un, but he kept putting off showing them to me. He stalled unmercifully, repeating material long learned and absorbed. I hinted that I was cognizant of the stall, and, that not availing, I cajoled him, recalling his earlier vow. This may have helped but drink did its part also, and about a week before I returned to the United States he marked K'un's spots on my body in a three-hour session. It was a typically hot and humid Taipei day, and after marking the spots and illustrating the tool for each spot, he would attempt to rub the spot out (we had used a marking pencil), but I was able to thwart these efforts. When we were through I rejected his offer of a bath, drove home and photographed them. Based on anatomy and time, they are too dangerous to delineate here. Suffice it to say that tien-hsueh holds that in the morning the most vulnerable target is the head; at midday, the upper torso; in the afternoon, from the navel to the knees; and in the evening, below the knees.

And so Hung I-hsiang: not a man to have over for learned discourse or a set of tennis, but I cannot imagine a better ally to have if things tended toward the physical.

2. The Monkey Boxer

One must toughen up without losing one's tenderness.   CHE GUEVARA

Liao Wu-ch'ang was all man. I never did learn his true age; reports put him in the range sixty-five to seventy-eight. When I arrived in Taiwan in 1959 he had four wives and eighteen children. He probably has more of both now. A fairly affluent traditional doctor, one of his sons was a Western-trained doctor of medicine. Liao had a half dozen shops throughout the city, was kept busy treating patients, and spent little time teaching boxing.

I met him by chance. Unhappy initially with Hung I-hsiang, I happened into a gift shop and asked the owner if he knew of a boxing teacher. Yes, he knew of one, but protocol had to be followed: he would see a friend of the boxer and tell me the next day. I purchased several things I did not need by way of thanks and left. When I returned the next day he introduced me to Peter Ch'en.

In my files there is a photograph of a Taiwanese man and his family. On the back is the legend, "To Mr. Smith—our friendship as sun bright, as sea deep," signed "Peter Ch'en." The photo shows a relaxed slender man and a rather pretty woman with two boys and a girl among their knees. Though not a boxer, he opened many doors all over Taiwan for me and did it without ever asking a penny. As I think of him after an absence of eleven years, I have recovered a bit of paper on which he wrote me a note. His terrible English (always, however, better than my Mandarin and non-existent Taiwanese) manages to convey the story of the Kaignan Temple. I paraphrase.

About two hundred years ago a Manchurian governed Taiwan. The capital was at Tainan city, and five families controlled the surrounding districts. The Shi family had the lumber monopoly. By means of rope fixed to each side, lumber was carried into the city, and anyone coming afoul of the carriers in the narrow street was knocked down. One day the carriers chanced upon a sixty-year-old man carrying salt. They swung the lumber against him but it failed to upend him. They struck him again but he only laughed. And again. Finally the old man pushed one antagonist on the shoulder, and blood issued forth from the man's mouth. It was then that the carriers realized that they had come across one of superior skills. The old man had two students who defeated some fighting monks some time afterward. A superior fighter from the ranks of the monks then beat the students, who lied to the old man about the circumstances of their defeat. The old man went to the temple, passed through the gate, and walked into the great hall (it was noticed that all the bricks on which he strolled were broken by his movement). The monks offered him a light for his pipe, but he refused and immediately levitated to the large lamp fixed to the roof, over twenty feet up. When they came to fight, the old man took off his upper garments, and the chief monk saw painted on his chest a dragon that indicated he was a brother boxer; thus was the fight aborted.

This kind of story is told and retold. I heard many such. I recall hours spent on Chinmen Island listening to a Cantonese tell me an

7–12. Liao Wu-ch'ang's Monkey Boxing

eerie eyewitness story of a ghost festival in a small village in Kwang⁄
tung Province, at which departed souls returned in their original
skins to do the boxing forms for which they were famous as well
as ones they had learned since shuffling off this mortal coil.

Peter Ch'en took me to Liao. I was immediately impressed. Don
Budge, in *Tennis the Professional Way*, asks rhetorically: "Which part
of an aging champion gives way first? The legs? The lungs?
The eyes? The reflexes? I feel definitely it's his stomach muscles. If
these are strong, the legs and arms will keep going." Liao had a flat
abdomen, which he would laughingly let me strike at will. He was
both lithe and blithe, and as deft as the red ant. Every morning at
3 A.M. he got up to take a cold bath, and this single act he felt was
the most important ingredient in his boyish health. This bath was
simply an abrupt overturning of a large basin of cold water over his
body—none of the gradualness of a shower turned slowly toward
cold. I had always put the cold water thesis in the category of
YMCA early chapel, bracing and fine but altogether ephemeral.
But Liao found it to be sustaining in overcoming the malnutrition
of the spirit afflicting all of us.

In truth he looked not over fifty, and he could do Monkey Boxing
(*ta sheng ch'uan*) off his knees faster and more beautifully than others
could do it at the normal level (figures 7–12). But then the low stuff
was his forte; jab, slash, thrust, and always to counter him you had
to find him. He was down there somewhere. And once found you

had to strike downward, which is not ideal for punches to retain their power. Okinawan and Japanese karateka had come to look at Liao's swift, knee-bouncing forms, and were awed by them. Yet, after studying for three years with him, I learned that none of it was very profound. It was simple south China Shao-lin coming out of Fukien and Kwangtung provinces a few centuries ago. But it was effective because of Liao's low posture, skill, and style. I learned at most only ten forms from him since we spent most of the time actually scrimmaging. Some of the forms I learned were: Monkey Boxing, Going along Three Roads, Three Offensives, Three Round Boxing, Small Four Gate Boxing, Side Cutting Boxing, and Cutting and Slashing.

Our rapport really deepened when my wife and I attended the wedding of one of his sons. At the party we were confronted with such Taiwanese delicacies as eels, white fungus soup, and sea slugs. We could have done one of two things: close our eyes and eat (and suffer later) or monopolize one of the few recognizable dishes, a boiled chicken, for the entire evening. We opted for the latter.

Although he could not have weighed more than 120 pounds, he was truly formidable. In pushing practice I could not move him until the late E. J. Harrison, the first Westerner to write in depth about Asian martial arts, told me of a similar fix he was in in Japan in the early years of this century. His master taught him to push upward instead of directly forward. I tried it, it worked. Liao smiled and said, "You found out, huh?" His specialty was low, shoe-top level stuff, involving much full squatting and jumps onto the inner leg surfaces. The movements were extremely fast, kicks were used infrequently, and, when done, focused low on the target. The open hand was used proportionally less than the closed fist, in a ratio of roughly 1 : 2.

We boxed several times weekly for the first year and at least once a week during the last two years. His back was always straight, and a favorite tactic (seen in most of his forms) was to fake high and come in low. He also tended toward counters, though he could initiate as well. He had trained under ten leading teachers and had served in añ advisory capacity with the local police. His knowledge of boxing was empirical; he learned it from the street. While I was there, he was still refereeing street fights, and, a native doctor, he was much sought after to treat the effects of these. He also gave me information on medicines to be taken internally or used externally and offered me a poison ring and knowledge on substances with which to poison the fingernails.[1]

Through Liao, other fighters, and books I learned about the esoteric science of attacking vital points (*tien hsueh*). A good but uneven text is Wan Lai-sheng's *Wu-shu Nei-wai-kung* (The Internal and External Fighting Arts). According to this source *tien hsueh* involves three kinds of spotting: striking spots, shutting spots, and grasping spots. Shao-lin theory holds that the human body contains 365 vulnerable ("soft") spots, 5 more than are used in acupuncture and moxibustion. Striking has 36 and shutting, 24 major points. The attack is oriented to twelve time periods of two hours each in the belief that the blood and neural activity is heaviest at these spots at specified times. Three families were traditionally famous in this art, the Yuan, Yang, and Kao. Lo Szu, a famous Shao-lin boxer, founded the Kao method, which stressed use of either the index finger alone or the index and middle finger together against soft spots. Although some of the points need only be touched, others required a strike. The one-finger attack, however, was the prime method; subtle and mysterious, the technique has largely been lost. Sometimes a victim of the "small hand" method would be touched and die later. After a touch on a vital point, no medicine could remedy. A person would die from a hit to the genitals in three days. Wan closes with advice on how to gain this ability: starting from a push-up off five fingers, one progresses to the point where he uses only the index finger of each hand as support while the toes rest on two bricks; then he is capable of spotting.

Or we may look into Chin I-ming's *Wu-tang Ch'uan-shu Mi Chueh* (Secrets of Wutang Boxing). Chin states that tien hsueh starts with training the fingertips. Next the vital soft spots are learned and equated to the times of blood circulation. Tien hsueh hand tech' niques used one/finger and two/finger tactics. These tactics divided into four: poking, slapping, pushing, and thrusting. The finger was stressed: it is the major weapon and can cause death. The palm was also used in slapping, pressing, and pushing, but this and the knees and elbows were tactics merely resulting in minor injuries.

To trace the art historically is impossible because of the secrecy attending it. Chin's research revealed that the first man famed for tien hsueh was named Shan Szu/nan. Shan taught Wang Cheng, who taught Huang Pai/chia. Huang named many of the spots as follows: death spot, dumb spot, dizzy spot, and cough spot (one not on this list is a spot that if hit purportedly causes the man struck to laugh himself to death).

Tien hsueh is complex and requires unremitting and meticulous study. Because it must be incorporated into regular boxing, one must first master boxing. Many masters were chary about passing the knowledge on and so died with their secrets. Even forty years ago when Chin was writing, the art was nearly extinct. Tien hsueh attempts to block the air and blood passages. In twenty/four hours the blood passes through twelve key parts of the body. The flow is not regular: sometimes it roars through the veins like a tidal wave, sometimes it seeps slowly. Spotting at a certain point at a certain time will cause stoppage and sometimes reversal of the flow.

The fingers may be trained by the mind, or in solo exercises against no resistance, or in practice using hard objects such as beans in a vase. Various parts of the hand may be trained for different purposes: the fingertips for touching or thrusting, the palm for slapping or hooking, or the hand/edge for chopping.

Master T'ang Tien/ch'in once said that the spotting of Chang San/feng, a Taoist priest of the Sung dynasty (960–1279), derived from that of another Taoist, Feng I/yuan. He had thirty/six targets. T'ang himself gave twenty/two frontal and twenty/two rear spots, all of which he claimed caused death. Ho Feng/ming, famed for tien hsueh, once referred to an "Eagle Claw" Wang, who was adept at grasping spots and who wrote a book on it. It was said that when Wang grasped someone that person immediately felt faint. Wang's training was exacting. He did the Yellow Dragon Clawing exercise, in which the fingers are rhythmically stretched and contracted for long periods. He next would place his hand in water that was brought to a boil. Then the hand was withdrawn and allowed to dry by itself. Following this he soaked the hand in an exotic mixture (the ashes of five pairs of eagle claws, elephant skin, turtle shells, herbs, and salt fried with ginger, wine, and vinegar left to set a month). Then he would thrust it into beans and stones. In this way, though the fingers looked normal, they could penetrate the stomach of a cow and bricks and timber.

It is said that Wang had 108 spots for his seizing techniques. Moreover, his action could be "released," that is, after he incapaci⁄tated someone he could relieve the affected part by another action. So we may assume that his seizing shut off veins and arteries, and his release merely reopened them.

Wang said that there is one major spot for every six inches of the body and one minor spot for every one⁄half inch. Every spot was governed by the time except two major ones (*jen, tu*); these two could be attacked anytime. Chin questions the idea of the time strike by quoting Master Ho Yu⁄shan: "To speak of spotting in accordance with time periods is deceitful; boxers used this to puzzle people."[2]

Some boxers experiment with live animals. Though the body structures differ, the major spots of animals and humans are similar, so it is relevant to conduct such tests. Chao Hai⁄p'ing, the senior student of Master Chiang Hsiu⁄yuan famed in Yunnan Province, once visited Chin and showed him a drawing of thirty⁄six spots on a horse. Chin ordered a horse to be brought in and spotted it accord⁄ing to the drawing. The horse fell over and did not recover for one⁄half hour.

Liao was also capable with the twin square rods, the sword, and other weapons. I have seen him take a wooden sword and slash cleanly through a piece of bamboo supported on the ends by paper— *without tearing the paper* (an alternative method was to place the bamʹ boo on two cups brimful of water and swipe through the bamboo without spilling a drop). This was real kung fu. I never approached his level in it.

There were other tricks used by the charlatans plying the medicine trade who called themselves boxers. Liao showed me some of these. A wire is stretched around the chest and the end knotted in such a way that chest expansion causes one part of the wire to cut the other part. A similar trick is to tie a rope around your chest and break it by inhalation. The rope is acid treated at one small place beforehand, and as you show it for inspection your hand holds (and disguises) the defective section. There were many others.

Nor are such things peculiar to Asia. John Clempert, a Russian wrestler, traveled with Houdini for a time billed as "The Man They Cannot Hang." Noosed, he would drop fifteen feet without injury. (A better feat than that performed by "Farmer" Burns, Frank Gotch's wrestling mentor, who was able to hang for half a minute in a noose.) Houdini himself was an example par excellence of a rigorously trained man able to perform feats requiring the utmost in agility and dexterity. In one of his old movies, I recall he was hung, his hands handcuffed behind his back, in a small room. With his legs he applied a scissors on the gangster's neck and choked him. Next, he kicked off his shoes and with his foot went through the man's pockets until he found the key to the handcuffs. Holding the key between his toes he unlocked them and, extricating himself, walked through the door a free man. Exaggeration surely, but it was indicative of his powers.

Beyond teaching me the fistic niceties, Liao opened up doors all over Taiwan for me.[3] I was welcomed by boxers who would not talk even to Chinese. The separation between the mainlanders and the Taiwanese on Taiwan is very real, but, through Liao, I was able to see nearly every Taiwanese master on the island. Later we discuss some of them, but one example here may not be amiss. Liao once took a friend and me to see an old Taiwanese boxer, Ch'en Ching⁄chang, who lived on a farm just off the road to Keelung and was reputed to have one⁄finger skill. He took us in his home, served tea, and set about his demonstration. First he put fuel oil on his right index finger, a gnarled, calloused digit much shorter than the one on his left hand, then lit it and let it burn. Next he put wine on the finger, scorched it black by holding it in the flame of a candle, and touched my colleague's lower back with the finger. My friend jumped from the pain. Next, he put more wine on the finger, and without prior burning lightly drew a line on my friend's lower back. The line turned red as if blood had been pulled to the surface by the finger. I tried the method on his left shoulder blade by hard pressure and succeeded not at all. My friend did it to himself near the original mark with pressure and did get a slight line, but this may have been the result of friction or scratching. The old man would not show what function the finger played in real fighting, nor would he demonstrate the kung fu used to put it in its present condition. Liao told me later that the man had killed a man fifteen years before and, out of remorse, had sworn never to teach his method. He had shown us only the power of the touch, not how to cultivate and use it.

This all too brief account of my time with Liao gives some of his fighting flavor but conveys little of his real gift—his sparkling approach to life. His boxing mitigated his penchant for tobacco and helped to keep him young and jumping in and out of pedicabs and gambling into the wee hours. But his omnipresent smile was even more of an indication of the total man. He perfectly exemplified the thought of the Irish author James Stephens (1882–1950):

> The top of being, or of art, isn't high seriousness, it is gaiety. Gaiety isn't humor—it is a kind of happiness, it is the infancy of happiness, and like every other art, it is a lost art.

The art is not a lost one. Liao Wu⁄chang was a master of it.

3. The Guerrilla General

Yuan Tao, a grand old man and a former guerrilla general, I met through the Taiwanese Peter Ch'en. Although one himself, he had little use for other mainlanders. He had lost property and some family members on the mainland, had been pensioned on a pittance by the Nationalists, and was somewhat embittered by it all. In his early sixties, he was still handsome and hardy, an older version of the wiry champion of Fukien Province during his army days in 1934 (figure 13). After a lengthy period of practicing with him at Peter Chen's house in the middle of Taipei (a city built for 250,000 and accommodating 1.5 million), I arranged for one of the three meetings each week to be held at my house on beautiful Yang Ming Mountain, a short distance outside the city. So every Thursday evening he

13. *Yuan Tao in 1934, when he won the Fukien Province championship*

would come to dine. A stalwart Christian, he would ask grace and even insist on bustling about the table parceling out the portions. After a time he became yeh-yeh ("grandfather") to my children.

Yuan believed in ch'i, but he did not believe in nurturing it by omphaloskepsis. He felt that correct practice in a sound form under an able teacher generated both ch'i and technique. One practiced boxing as he lived his life. He thought Sir James M. Barrie was right ("It's grand, and you canna expect to be baith grand and com-fortable"), that a man developed from the tests he put his body to. This discipline is, of course, a universal: Saint Francis of Sales would not permit himself to sit comfortably even when alone, and Jacques Bossuet, seventeenth-century archbishop of Meaux, once traveled in a post chaise from Paris to Calais without once leaning back in the seat.

The ch'i, he said, was a power, an energy, but it could never make a man superhuman—only supernormal. The old myths were so much trash. Killing from a distance was only legend kept alive by unsophisticated people who saw a boxer beat another with a short strike so rapid as to be unobserved. Contact was necessary. But for the plodding shoulder-locked fisting of karate he had little use. A strike should be fast, meshed with the body weight, and speedily retracted it if is to be effective.

Once the high-ranking Korean karate master Shon Duk-sung came to my house and, after a meal, offered to show his skill. He performed a variety of defensing techniques on me, and all the while Yuan and several other boxers shook their heads. I did not find his art superior or novel; even less did the Chinese boxers. Later "Young" Ch'en approached Shon and challenged him, but the Korean refused, saying he had come to Taiwan to learn, not to fight. Yuan told me that Shon was too slow, and while karate looked good, it had little utility in actual fighting. The wrestler Shang T'ung-sheng, who seldom spoke, did so on this occasion, noting that karate was rudimentary Shao-lin suitable only for children.

I learned the long Yang T'ai-chi method from Yuan at the same

⑭ *14. Yuan teaching T'ai-chi*

time I was learning it from Wang Yen-nien (figure 14). Under Yuan it was straighter and less athletic. He thought Cheng Man-ch'ing did not make enough use of the shoulders (Cheng was against the segmented approach, preferring to develop power from his legs).

Yuan's ideas on boxing history were interesting. He believed that there had been a Buddhist Shao-lin Temple in Fukien, at Chuan-chou, that T'ai-chi originated in the Ming dynasty and Hsing-i earlier from Yueh Fei, a Sung-dynasty general.[1] He had met Sun Lu-t'ang, whom he regarded as a minor boxer but a good politician, in the late 20s or early 30s. It was significant, said he, that Chang Tzu-chiang, and not Sun, was elected president of the Chinese Boxing Association in Nanking. The Nanking association had experimented with all forms of fighting. Western boxing, which had a vogue in Shanghai, was studied, and the jabs and punches to the head, absent from Chinese boxing, were incorporated.

Besides T'ai-chi, I learned his method of Hsing-i, which he said had been taught him by the famed Wu Yun-t'ing. The method departs significantly from the orthodox style shown by the same master in his book, however. Thus it must be regarded as a modifi-cation, but an excellent one. In his Hsing-i the groin is always protected. *Peng-ch'uan* ("crushing") shows the difference. Whereas in the orthodox method the standing fist is delivered from a straight posture, in Yuan's style it is done from a curved, lower posture and done essentially with the index and middle finger of the fist. I had learned the orthodox method from Paul Kuo and Wang Shu-chin but found Yuan's style more satisfying. Yuan often would hold the posture for fifteen minutes.

Novel also was his *liang-i,* which he had learned from Ch'i Chin-ho and Wei Fang-shih in Tai-ho, Anhwei, the only place it was taught on the mainland. This form stressed leg and shoulder power and a double impact to each punch. One arm is used for balance and leverage at the instant the other strikes. The rear arm also lets one reserve some power, so as to counter the counter if need be. Yuan had learned it from the age of ten.

Yunnan lien pu ch'uan (Consecutive Step Yunnan Boxing) was another of his favorites. This is a standardized form, mainly Shao-lin but tinted with some of the internal forms, which was taught Nation-alist troops during World War II. An extremely rational form, it incorporates hand, fist, elbow, and shoulder strikes; pushing; locking; and advancing and retreating methods. Significantly, it has only one foot technique. Although he taught me fourteen leg movements, Yuan believed that kicking is only effective if done in conjunction with the hands and if kept low. Even on low kicks the attacker must keep the leg as low as possible and retract the foot swiftly.

With some other Shao-lin, joint forms, ch'in-na, and stick methods behind us, Yuan launched me last on free hand and foot exercises synthesized from all methods of Chinese boxing. These movements show no guard; they occur immediately with the op-ponent's attacks. When the enemy attacks the relaxed hands and body immediately counter. His ability with these was what made Yuan a provincial champion in his younger days. Even on the shady side of sixty his short, seemingly light strikes hurt my arms more than the burly punches of far bigger and much younger men.

One of the best swordsmen on Taiwan, Yuan also could handle the stick beautifully. Doug Bone, a *bo-jutsu* adept from Japan, found he knew little when crossing staffs with the oldster. The key here was the screwing effect achieved by turning the wrist inward concomitant with the strike.

Yuan knew no English, and my imperfect grasp of Chinese left me getting but half of his meaning, but in boxing, as in love, the words are not too important. I may forget some of his teaching, but will never forget the strong yet gentle man himself. Philip Marlowe in his last great adventure is queried by a woman: the woman won-ders how such a hard man can be so gentle. Marlowe responds: "If I wasn't hard, I wouldn't be alive. If I couldn't ever be gentle, I wouldn't deserve to be alive." Yuan Tao had those twin qualities— and in real life, where it is infinitely harder than it is in fiction.

4. Master of the Five Excellences

*A civilized Chinese is the most civilized per,
son in the world.*   BERTRAND RUSSELL

Before launching an exposition of the teaching of Cheng Man,
ch'ing, the most profound I encountered, it may be well to capsulize
what the art he taught, T'ai,chi, involves.[1] T'ai,chi is a Taoist
exercise, a moving form of meditation, which gives the vision (Wil,
liam Blake called it "imagination") through which to see Truth.
This vision has nothing to do with the eyes. In fact, the philosopher
Chuang Tzu, a contemporary of Mencius, said, "The eye envies the
mind." Here I list what I regard as the essentials of the art. With
these as background, we then can go on to the remarkable man
teaching this remarkable art.

1. T'ai,chi Ch'uan ("Grand Ultimate Boxing") is an ancient
form of Chinese slow,motion calisthenics and self,defense
(which is fast becoming popular in the West). As physical
exercise it can be practiced by all—young and old, male and
female—without the restrictions of weather, space, time, cloth,
ing, or equipment common to other sports.
2. There are four theories on the origin of T'ai,chi. The most
popular (and the one Cheng Man,ch'ing subscribes to) states that
Chang San,feng learned it in a dream. A second theory claims
that it originated in the T'ang dynasty (618–ca. 907) and devel,
oped through the merged teachings of four schools: the Hsu, Yu,

Ch'eng, and Yin. A third claim says that the Ch'en family of Ch'en Chia Kou in Honan Province created it during the Ming dynasty (1368–1644). The fourth, and most reasonable, thesis simply avers that the founder of T'ai-chi is unknown, but that its development dates from one Wang Chung-yueh of Shansi Province, who introduced it in Honan. (See appendix A.)

3. T'ai-chi stresses slow, deep breathing and balanced, relaxed postures (*kung chia*). For an investment of ten to forty minutes a day (the 128-posture round requires twenty minutes; the 37-posture round, seven minutes to perform), the solo exercise promises to promote health and prolong life.

4. First, last, and always the student must relax. Various calisthenics aid him in achieving this. All rigidity and strength must be emptied from the upper torso and must sink to the very soles of the feet, one of which is always firmly rooted to the ground (figure 15). Without proper relaxation the student can never hope to achieve the trueness of the T'ai-chi postures. The student relaxes completely and breathes as a child—naturally through the nose, the diaphragm being aided by the abdominal rather than the intercostal muscles. Man's intrinsic energy, the ch'i, should be stored just below the navel. The mind directs this energy throughout the body according to need.[2] But the ch'i cannot circulate in an unrelaxed body.

5. The waist is the foundation of all bodily movement. It is the big axis from which all T'ai-chi movements derive their

15. *Cheng Man-ch'ing rooting and thwarting the push of four men*

celerity, crispness, and power. Only in the flexibility of the waist is there true strength. To fight with arms or legs inde-pendently of the waist is the mark of the perpetual beginner.

6. The earliest classic on T'ai-chi stresses that when the lowest vertebrae are straight, the spirit of vitality reaches to the top of the head and that when the head is held as if suspended from above, the entire body will feel light and nimble. The body must be held "so lightly that the addition of a feather will be felt, and so pliable and sensitive that a fly cannot alight on it without setting it in motion."[3]

7. After mastering the basic solo exercise and auxiliary calis-thenics, the student advances to pushing hands (t'ui shou) practice with a partner. Here he learns to interpret his oppo-nent's moves, to yield before him, and to defeat him by "neutral-izing a thousand pounds with four ounces." He learns the true significance of the fundamentals embodied in the solo exercise.

8. The pushing-hands practice develops into a comprehensive method of self-defense. Aikido and a few other Asian methods emphasize the yielding principle of T'ai-chi, but none achieves to the same degree its relaxation, subtlety, and suppleness. By mastering the ch'i, many T'ai-chi exponents are able to with-stand the full power of fist or foot.

9. T'ai-chi develops a tenacious strength quite different from the force associated with most fighting arts. Tenacity may be likened to a strong vine that is pliable; force, to a stick that is rigid. Tenacity comes from the sinews; force, from the bones. Tenacity is always to be preferred, because it springs from the ch'i. Sound boxing is rooted in the feet, sprouts in the legs, is directed by the waist, and functions through the fingers.

10. Every movement in correct boxing contains circles. (G. K. Chesterton put it well: "I find that most round things are nice, particularly Eternity and a baby.") If you are attacked on a straight line and you resist with a straight line defense, the

stronger force will prevail. But if the incoming force is neutralized by circularity, it is a simple matter to defeat an opponent, regardless how strong. Say you are attacked with one
hundred pounds of force frontally. Using T'ai-chi, you with-
draw slightly and neutralize your opponent's rush. If he cannot
check his momentum he will go over his toes. A slight pull is
enough to bring him down. If, however, he sees his error, checks
his forward impetus, and withdraws backward, the incoming
and outgoing forces cancel each other, and, by applying but
five pounds of force on the line of his retreating body, you will
topple him easily.

11. Correct teaching, perseverance, and natural talent are required. However, the first two requirements are the most
important. A master is not made in twenty minutes a day.
Mastery comes from decades, not years, of meshing the T'ai-chi
postures and the state of mind they develop with every movement of every day. Abdominal breathing and a relaxed body
through every minute are prerequisites. If these habits are coupled with unremitting daily practice with all varieties of part-
ners, excellence will emerge.

While I was lunching with a Chinese friend in Tainan one day,
he told me of a famous Chinese artist who knew T'ai-chi, a "strange"
man named Cheng Man-ch'ing. I looked for and found the man
and knocked at his door seeking instruction. Among some Ori-
entals giving is a privilege that has to be earned. When I first
met Cheng, I did not know this, and I showered him liberally
with gifts. My motive was immediate tuition. He accepted the
gifts but not their substance: me. Instead, in the accepted Chinese
fashion, he assigned me for a year to Liang Tung-tsai, a senior
student and teacher in his own right.

Liang had been near death from a liver ailment in 1950. Hearing
of the famed Cheng Man-ch'ing, he approached him, learned
T'ai-chi, regained his health, and sat at his feet thereafter. A retired

customs official, he came to the United States in the middle sixties, and is now teaching T'ai-chi in Boston.

Without asking a penny, Liang taught me the thirty-seven pos- tures (*kung chia*) and introduced me to both the philosophy of the art and many fine boxers, including Wang Yen-nien, another well- known T'ai-chi teacher, for pushing-hands practice. Liang's ap- proach on this was simply to improve my root and defense, so that when Cheng was ready for me I would have a good basis for learn- ing offense. This proved an excellent tactic. Subsequently, Liang introduced me to Han Ch'ing-t'ang, the ch'in-na expert (see chap- ter 7).

While I was practicing with Liang, he told me much of Cheng, the man of the "Five Excellences" (painting, poetry, calligraphy, medicine, and T'ai-chi). In 1925 Cheng, a professor of art in two universities in Peking, was in an advanced stage of tuberculosis, which forced him to go south to the Shanghai College of Arts and Chi-nan University, where he founded the College of Fine Arts. But his malady worsened and he was on the point of death when a friend introduced him to Yang Ch'eng-fu, one of the greatest T'ai-chi masters in China. All else had failed, so Cheng began T'ai-chi. In his words: "Within a few months the internal hemor- rhage stopped and my temperature returned to normal. In a year or so my illness was completely defeated."

After a year of learning the basic postures from Liang and the pushing-hands practice from Wang Yen-nien (while practicing other forms of boxing), I knocked again, and this time Cheng Man- ch'ing opened the door. I found a short slight man, who, with hands as fine as a lady's, took my arm and led me into the house. There he gave me my first lesson, telling me to relax and to quiet my mind. (Karlfried von Durckheim, one of the leading European authorities on mind-body synthesis, notes that in all spiritual exercises everything is contained in the very first lesson.) Because of the greater develop- ment of muscle sense and the improved circulation that accompanies greater organic efficiency, the physically fit person can relax more completely than the one in poor physical condition. But one must be trained in relaxation. There is nothing mystical in such training. One simply perseveres in the postures and in pushing-hands.

For more than two years thereafter I was honored by being made a member of the advanced group of students who assembled at the master's home every Sunday morning for several hours. And in the last six months of my stay Cheng permitted me an additional after-noon of private practice each week. Practice was what one made it. I worked very hard and at first was forever being bounced off the wall. I minded this not and was only disturbed when Cheng would intercede with some husky to save me some knocks. I preferred to settle such things myself.

But it was not merely, or even primarily, to spare me pain that he interfered. He pointed out that I perspired too much, that the ch'i thus escaped, that one must win by relaxing. And so a pause was in order. Coming from the judo experience, I was prepared to sweat and exert till mastery came. But it does not come thus in T'ai-chi, Cheng said; it comes by "quiet minding" while "investing in loss." And it comes with time.

On the other hand, some of my more zealous attackers also had a lesson to learn. More than once Cheng, sensing the proceedings trending toward the sadistic, would wave me aside and "play" with my antagonist. The attacker would find the roles reversed and him-self the object of hands that transmitted energy that shocked rather than merely shook. The short and sweet lesson here (and later when I was more proficient and overly zealous I relearned it) was that one should not be greedy; when playing with an inferior, respect him.

This is not to say that T'ai-chi does not require effort. It does. But it requires quite as much faith. I asked Cheng once why none of his students approached him in skill. His terse answer: "No faith." Faith in what? Simply in the twin principles *relax* and *sink*, in not resisting and always remaining gently attached to the opponent.

Cheng said that he had left the secret of T'ai-chi out of his *Cheng-tzu T'ai-chi Ch'uan Shih-san P'ien* (Cheng's Thirteen Chapters on

T'ai-chi Boxing) to prevent the outside world from getting it. It was simply this: never put more than four ounces of energy on your opponent and never let him put more than four ounces on you. Indeed the old axiom of defeating one thousand pounds with four ounces of trigger force means that you never receive one thousand pounds. If this is followed, Cheng said, mastery will come. Few follow it.

In pushing, he said, it is well to keep in mind that if the man opposing you is stiff, it is an easy matter to push him. If he is relaxed, it is more difficult. Against the first, you may push without preliminary. But against a relaxed person, one touches lightly, and only when one detects a wave of resistance is the push applied. This is called *t'i fang* (lift-let go). As you touch the opponent in your attempt to elicit resistance, inhale to the sole of your foot with your mind. Then as you exhale all your power comes from the sole, rather than the hands. If you use hand strength you will break your own root. To achieve success, you must relax everything. The waist is relaxed by straightening the spine naturally and willing the relaxation. The thigh and leg are much more difficult to relax, but they should also be relaxed as much as possible if the energy triggered from the sole is to be transmitted without interruption to the fingertips.

Cheng told me that energy must not be generated from the shoulders and chest. At first it should come from the middle spine. Work to lower it from here to the sacrum, thence to the sole. The further down it goes, the greater the power is. Because the ability to transmit ch'i from the sole of one foot up through the fingers takes decades, intermediate linkages must be used as follows:

> hip — shoulder
> knee — elbow
> ankle — wrist
> sole — palm

In pushing hands, when your weight is on the rear leg, bring your power from the sacrum; when your weight is on the front leg, the energy need is less and power from the middle spine area is adequate. There are many kinds of energy (see Ch'en Yen-ling's *T'ai-chi Ch'uan Tao Chien Kan San-shou Ho-pien* [T'ai-chi Boxing, with Broadsword, Sword, Stick, and Free Hands Techniques]), but most are not of a high order. An example of this skill is vibratory energy, in which the entire body spasmodically trembles. It is excellent against a man holding you from the rear but may cause him serious internal injury.

Simply observing the art without participating in it can be misleading. I once made the mistake of taking an American *nidan* in Okinawan karate to meet Cheng. The American was singularly unimpressed by what he saw. He wanted a test. So Cheng signaled to a student, who then faced the karateka. He faked a high kick, the student's arm started up; the foot flashed down, the student slapped it lightly while stepping inside and touching the American's heart. Dead, he failed to realize it, for he went away scoffing at T'ai-chi. I apologized to Cheng later and he waved it aside: "One must be kind to blind men." The inevitable sequel: I took the lad to a Shaolin friend of mine and left him to his ministrations. A week later I saw him. He had discontinued. Why? "Damn it, those guys wanted to fight!" Unappreciative of the soft, afraid of the hard, this one doubtless is still thrilling them at cocktail parties with his dance. Fighting it is not.

Cheng emphasized a sound foundation, saying that a good teacher, a good system, and a healthy body could not but beget success. Lacking any of these, the results would be less. All the great masters had this sound foundation from which their great skills emerged. From Cheng and his circle I heard of masters having such skills. The father of modern T'ai-chi, Yang Lu-ch'an, who practiced past seventy years of age, once walked several blocks through the rain and mud to visit a friend. But when he arrived at his friend's house, he had no trace of mud on his shoes! The same friend also claimed to have seen Yang's son, Pan-hou, do this trick once. Pan-hou also reportedly levitated in the friend's presence. Yang's other son, Chien-hou, would let a swallow stand on his open palm. The bird could not fly away because Chien⁄hou, "hearing" his energy, would yield subtly so that it would not have a base from which to fly. Chien⁄hou also once defeated a famed swordsman with a small brush.[4] Li Pin⁄fu, who studied under Wang Lang⁄t'ing (a prized student of Yang Lu⁄ch'an; he died early), was once challenged by a robust southerner who, having *ch'i⁄kung* skill (see appendix C), could push chairs and tables without touching them. Li was past sixty and, holding a dog cradled in his left arm, attempted to refuse, but the boxer attacked anyhow. Li deftly knocked the man down without relinquishing his gentle hold on the dog.

Few of these skills have come down to the present, though there are many who claim to possess them. It sometimes went to absurd lengths. I met one man who had published a book on the benefits of increasing ch'i by attaching weights to the genitalia. Another T'ai⁄chi advocate, a professor at the ordnance college, once had a part in a public display I attended. He began by stating that his ch'i prevented anyone from taking his writing brush from his fingers as he wrote.[5] (In one of his books Nikos Kazantzakis tells how an acquaintance was able to survive the cold and starvation of depression Berlin in the 1920s by practicing breathing while doing calligraphy, the brush and elbow lined up with his heart.) He challenged anyone to come forward and attempt to pull it from his fingers. A nondescript soldier came forth smiling and promptly pulled the brush from him. A titter rose through the audience as the professor explained that either he was not ready or the soldier had done it incorrectly. They would do it again. But again the soldier pulled the brush from the "ch'i⁄powered fingers." The professor began explaining why it had happened a second time, but by this time the pragmatic audience was roaring. In the midst of his unheard explanation, the next demonstration began in back of him, and he walked off the stage smiling uneasily. This seemed to me rash discourtesy on the part of the audience but shows their independence and pragmatism.

This does not mean that ch'i is not real, only that some who pre⁄

tend to have this skill in reality do not. Cheng indeed is a living rep-
resentation of it. He told me that Taoists explain it this way:

> According to Chinese medical theory, the secretion of certain
> organs mixed in the kidneys forms an essence called *ching*. One
> tries to conserve the *ching* by sexual abstinence and to vaporize
> it into ch'i. This is done mainly in the "sea of ch'i" the *tan-t'ien*,
> 1.3 inches below the navel and three-tenths of the distance
> toward the spine. The main force is the mind, which concen-
> trates on the *tan-t'ien*. The ch'i is breathed in and combines with
> the *ching* in the *tan-t'ien*, thus creating heat. The inspired ch'i
> (the *t'ien-ch'i*) thus becomes *yuan-ch'i*, an electrical substance,
> which travels through the blood vessels and enters the bone
> structure through the sacrum. Since the bone has no other open-
> ing, the hot ch'i inside the bone becomes like steam and, on
> cooling, becomes bone marrow. The marrow when full pushes
> up to the brain, the "sea of marrow." At that time the spirit is
> full, the man is a complete man.

The proof of ch'i was Cheng, but there was other evidence. Hsih
Shu-fung, a sixty-five-year-old student of his from Taichung, several
times asked me to strike him anywhere I wished (except in the head
and genitals). As I struck him, the impact sent his 105 pounds back
into the arms of two men, who shoved him back to me. I hit him
twenty to twenty-five times in the solar plexus and chopped under
his arms and over his heart with great vigor. He took it all in good
humor, smiling. A Chinese former Western boxing middleweight
champion of Shanghai also hit him to no avail. Hsih had learned
T'ai-chi from Cheng some years before and with time had developed
this ability to take a punch. Another of Cheng's students, William
Ch'en, also had this ability (see page 76). But of all the boxers I
punched freely only these two, both T'ai-chi adepts, took the punches
in a relaxed manner. Pa-kua master Wang Shu-chin (see page 72)
was famous for this, but, although relaxed, he had such a belly that it
seemed a qualitatively different thing.

And such skills come unevenly. One practitioner, the daughter of a former Chinese ambassador to the United States, came a few times to observe the practice. I was there the day she told Cheng of Li Huang/tze, her T'ai/chi master in Shanghai. Cheng nodded that he knew the man. The woman then said he had special powers. Cheng asked her to explain. She told how she had tired of pushing hands and asked him what he would do against a real attack. He urged her to attack. She approached, attacking him; as she neared him a force propelled her back, and she began bouncing up and down. When her feet began to hurt she implored him to let her stop. With a pass of his hand, he permitted her to stop bouncing. She also said that when he touched a student his hands generated sparks. Cheng laughed at all this. "I knew Li," he said. "His T'ai/chi was not too good. He could do the thing you mention but only because you are a student. The trick will not work against an equal or a superior." Cheng later told me that Li had learned T'ai/chi from Tung Yin/chieh (another senior student of Yang Ch'eng/fu) and subsequently had gained a special skill of "knocking down without touching." The skill depended on student awe, however, and would not work against a good boxer.

Once while enjoying a lingering hour, I mentioned to Cheng that Franklin Kwong, a T'ai/chi classmate, had told me of two men in Shanghai whom he had seen knock down men from a distance without contact. Kwong was an engineer, graduated from New York University, and not likely to be taken in by charlatans. Did Cheng believe such a thing was possible? He responded that he had heard of those two masters but had never met them. Not having seen them he could not verify that they possessed such a skill. Sig/nificantly, neither would he say they had not achieved such mastery.

While keeping an open mind on such things (E. J. Harrison, my old friend, described in 1913 in *The Fighting Spirit of Japan* seeing Kunishige, a *kiaijutsu* adept, drop a man with a shout), it is well to recall the story of a guru who sent his prize student off to the Hima/layas for advanced instruction. Twelve years later the student returns,

16–21. Cheng dodging a blow and retaliating by uprooting

and the first day back goes walking with the guru. They come to a river. Thinking to impress the old man, the student walks across the water to the opposite shore. The guru pays a copper and is boated across. When he alights from the boat, he is accosted by the student: "Why did you take a boat?"

To which the guru quietly countered, "Why did you study for twelve years just to save a copper?"

Cheng always stressed that the body of the art is much more important than its mere function. If the body is mastered, he said, the function cannot but be automatic and effective (figures 16–21). The function was useful but unimportant. More important were the concepts of four ounces, investing in loss, relaxing, sinking, and rooting. Often he himself was at a loss to explain the use of a certain posture: down the corridors of time he had lost it somewhere. I can recall him stating that Wave Hands in Clouds, one of the thirty-seven postures, is for waist use, and can function as either a feint or a deflection and finger-thrust attack while the body rolls horizontally.

He equated the foot attacks to the five elements as follows:

Element	Quality	Posture
Water	soft, round	Turn Body and Sweep Lotus with Leg
Wood	straight, piercing	Separate the Foot
Fire	terrible	Turn and Strike with Heel
Metal	hard	Golden Cock Stands on One Leg
Earth	rising power	Squatting Single Whip

He spoke seldom of tien hsueh, but when he did it was invariably profound. On the mainland he had been attacked once by famed Wu Meng/hsia, and Cheng had injured him. Wu specified "three years," meaning that they would have another go three years later. Because Wu was a formidable opponent, Cheng respected him enough to study tien hsueh (see pages 9, 15) intensively with two famous masters for five years. As it turned out, Wu never returned. Cheng felt the time spent was nonetheless beneficial despite the fact that he had only half an art: he learned only the injurious part. He would have had to spend double the time to learn special means of correcting the effect of strikes.

It is not that the functions contained in T'ai/chi are not themselves effective. When you are attacked use *peng* to parry and attack with. If he pushes your arm, use *che tieh* ("folding," a technique mentioned in the *T'ai/chi Boxing Classics*). Keeping the arm supple, when the opponent pushes your elbow, relax the elbow and hit him with your hand; if he pushes your hand, fold and hit him with your elbow. This shows interplay of yin and yang and is quite effective.

Cheng's teacher, Yang Ch'eng/fu, was said to be friendly—compared with his older brother Yang Shao/hou. Several boxers on Taiwan told me that they had had friends killed by the latter. These stories are hardly credible, but certain it is that Yang Shao/hou was a harsh teacher.[6] However, according to Cheng, Yang Ch'eng/fu was not all that nice either. A big man from the north, he had an illustrious name. During training he practiced the Single Whip for expansive power and Play the Guitar for contractive power, holding each statically for lengthy periods. He also moved repeatedly through Step Back and Repulse the Monkey (for moving the ch'i up past the sacrum) and Step Forward, Deflect Downward, Parry, and Punch. But mostly he sat and seldom spoke. The students were afraid to ask him questions. Their fear may have resulted from seeing what happened to Cheng when he approached Yang for some pushing-hands practice. Yang used two fingers and threw him twenty feet, knocking him out. When the memory of this faded, Cheng approached him again. This time Yang put a hand (Cheng remembers that it was as soft as cotton) on his jaw, threw him and knocked him out. These were the only two times Cheng faced Yang.

If this is true, whence came Cheng's great ability? The senior students around Yang would have nurtured some of it. Much probably came from Chang Ch'ing-ling, a farmer who, it is said, could root so well that his feet sank into the ground. Chang was actually trained by Yang Pan-hou, making him a boxing "brother" of Yang Ch'eng-fu, but for some reason the Yang family wanted him inscribed as a student of Yang Ch'eng-fu. He was an exceptional fighter. Once a famous boxer, Wan Lai-sheng, came and challenged Yang's circle. Chang met the challenge, but the fight went nowhere: both injured their hands at the outset and it was postponed. Years later when Chang had achieved some fame he traveled about challenging leading boxers. He went undefeated until he braced a Taoist surnamed Dzou and was tumbled immediately. Dzou commented, "Your technique, sir, is none too good." Chang stayed with this man a while and derived a new method of doing the postures.

Chang probably taught Cheng a great deal; some believe his incredible ability in pushing hands comes largely from Chang. However, there is another explanation. In Szechwan, Cheng met a Taoist and studied under him, after which, according to Ch'en Wei-ming, his skill increased greatly. I asked Cheng about this at least three times from different strategic angles, and each time he drew a veil over it. He was little better on questions regarding Chang's contribution, always saying, "I got it from Yang Ch'eng-fu." It remains a mystery.

Yang Ch'eng′fu's laziness and pedagogical obtuseness during the period Cheng studied under him is fairly characteristic of many masters.[7] Ch'en Wei′ming tells how Yang Lu′ch'an beat all of T'ai′chi master Ch'en Ch'ang′hsing's students, and was invited by the master to come to him for special instruction. Next day Yang went. Ch'en sat in a chair and appeared to be either asleep or sick. His head lolled uncomfortably to one side. Yang supported his head till his arms ached. Finally Ch'en appeared to awaken. He curtly told Yang he was too tired, and that he should return on the morrow. Next day Yang returned. Ch'en again appeared to be asleep. When he finally awoke, Yang still sat, respectful. Again Ch'en begged off, telling him to come back on the next day. Yang did and a wide′ awake Ch'en then agreed to teach him. He had passed the test.

Cheng Man′ch'ing, raised in the culture and wanting the skill so badly, was prepared to put up with anything to get it. He saw the vistas open to him if he persisted. He saw Yang lazy and growing fat but still unbeatable. During this period he saw Yang easily defeat famed boxer Wu Hui′pei. And once, walking with Yang, they were run into from the rear by a pedicab. The cab hit Yang squarely and rebounded ten feet, tipping over and spilling its occupants on the ground—the result of "receiving energy." Yang scarcely was aware of the incident, continuing his conversation through it all.

Later, Cheng himself stood in Hunan Province and took on all challengers. During this period the famous master Tu Hsin′wu visited him for a friendly match; Cheng found that everywhere he turned Tu's foot caught him. As a teen′ager, Cheng said, Tu was already highly skilled and taught others. A dwarf named Hsu hung around Tu's group but never showed anything. He once berated Tu to others for smoking opium. Tu heard of this, was angered, but said nothing. Later he attempted to ambush Hsu on a narrow bridge. The dwarf dodged and pushed Tu off the bridge but saved him a nasty fall by catching him by the pigtail and exclaiming, "You are a strange boy. You smoke opium and now you try to kill me!" Tu then bowed before Hsu and asked him to teach him.

In Chungking, Cheng was matched with the famed Wan Lai-sheng, but this bout never took place because of the war. During the same period, in an exhibition at the British embassy in Chung-king, he was laughed at by some Britishers for his slightness. Ch'en Wei-ming asked the laughers if they wanted to have a go. He got a unanimous response. The most robust chap approached Cheng and asked what style of fighting he would prefer. Cheng replied, "As you wish." The Britisher swung a right fist from ten feet. Cheng neutralized it and pushed him down. He got up and tried his left with the same result. Then, very angry, he surged up and drove both fists at the face of the little man. Cheng evaded, put his right palm on the big one's left armpit and pushed him more than ten feet away, and, following him to the edge of the platform, caught him, saving him serious injury.

Still later Cheng went to Taiwan. There he wanted to advance from the first step of the third (Heaven) stage of skill.[8] This required that he go into seclusion for intensive meditation. He began this regimen, but his family required his aid, and he was forced to return to Taipei and mundane affairs. If it is true that Cheng when he came to Taiwan wanted to retire from society so that his art would ascend, this seems to imply that the art we have is incomplete, that it needs supplementing with other forms of Taoist meditation. But some there are (Liang Tung-tsai is one) who believe that the art is suffi-cient. Liang told me that Yang Lu-ch'an, Ch'en Ch'ing-p'ing (mid-nineteenth century), and other greats had reached the summit of the art without Taoist meditation. Indeed, Liang said, the *T'ai-chi Boxing Classics* is very explicit on the point:

> Diligent practice brings the skill of interpreting strength. From this the ultimate goal is complete mastery of detecting the op-ponent's strength . . . Coordinating the solid and empty is the key here. If that is achieved, then you can interpret strength. After this, by studying vigorously and remembering, one can reach the stage of total reliance on the mind.

From this, Liang argued persuasively that T'ai-chi embraces within it all the conditions of Taoist meditation. I heard that Yang Lu-ch'an was once ambushed by one hundred men and, not wanting to kill any of the miscreants, he wrapped his cloak about him, sub-mitted to the beating, and was left for dead. The next day Yang worked as usual, but many of his attackers took to their beds as a result of injuries received from beating the cloaked Yang. I scoffed at this example of the summit, but Cheng urged me not to; even he with but a part of Yang's energy had once permitted a famed Shao-lin boxer to strike his relaxed arm. The boxer struck once and withdrew. When asked why, he told his friends that his entire side had been paralyzed on contact with Cheng's arm. Indeed, Wan Lai-sheng writes that when the arms and legs are no longer needed, when the ch'i holds sway, one is invulnerable to even knives and spears. This is called "Gold Bell Cover" (*chin chung chao*).

Back in circulation in Taiwan, Cheng soon had a large group of students. And again he was vulnerable to challenges. One such occurred when a well-known praying mantis style boxer, Liang Tzu-p'eng, came from Hong Kong to Taiwan to try conclusions with the locals. He traded punches (the accepted challenge method) with a leading Pa-kua-Hsing-i teacher, and his free punch put the local man down to his knees. In turn, the local boxer did not hurt Liang with his punch, so the affair had to be adjudged in Liang's favor. Strutting out of the park where this occurred, Liang asked if Taiwan had any other boxers. Someone mentioned Cheng's name, so Liang accosted Cheng at a party. Cheng resisted the challenge, saying that the place and time were inappropriate. Liang persisted until Cheng invited him to his house a day or so later. Liang came and watched Cheng's demonstrations of T'ai-chi dynamics. But he was not satisfied. "This is interesting," Liang said, "but what would you do if I attacked you?" Cheng replied that he would attempt to push him away. Liang, by this time convinced that the small man before him was afraid to fight, retorted that it would be well to get ready for he was about to attack.

At this point, Cheng said, "Very well, but if you even see my hands move I'll never call myself Cheng again" (to give up one's name is so serious that many Chinese would commit suicide rather than do it). Liang attacked from fifteen feet with a combined foot-fist action. Those watching did not see what happened, only the result. Liang first was on top of Cheng striking, next he was propelled backward by an unseen force and bounced off the wall unconscious.

Those who were there will never forget it. Liang himself took it in good grace, stayed on and studied T'ai-chi for a time. But before he went back to Hong Kong he returned to the park to see the man he had defeated earlier. That one casually told Liang that he was getting ready to challenge Cheng Man-ch'ing. Liang said, "Don't bother. I've already been there."

Once Cheng invited me to attack him in any way I wished. From long years of judo and boxing I thought I knew how to maintain balance. I thought. I faked high with my hands and went in low to push his midriff. But he was not there when I arrived. Holding his hands lightly on mine he avoided my attack and in the same movement I bounced off the wall. I tried repeatedly, but never once did I penetrate his posture. His feet moved very little, but the acute sensitivity of his body to my touch permitted him to neutralize me and push and lead me at will. Often he drew me forward so sharply that my ear nearly grazed the ground, and then, at the last moment, he would catch me, saving me some nasty consequences. His art goes beyond technique; I have never experienced anything so relaxed and yet so frighteningly efficient in my life.

Another time he invited me to attack him. I did. He dodged in, deflected, struck me lightly. He had done this before. But this time he did not stop the attack. Both hands were in my eyes, on my throat, all over my midriff and at the same time his feet peppered my legs. It was so beautifully orchestrated that I could not turn from it. I backed frantically until I came to the wall, where, after taking his finger from my throat, he desisted. Informal and friendly it should have been, but frightening is what it actually was. Against that there was no defense. I am certain that no one has ever been struck more quickly and often in such a short span of time. Fortunately, he put little energy into the strikes.

22. *Sun Lu-t'ang, a famous T'ai-chi master*

Cheng associated little with other boxers. Like Sun Lu-t'ang, "His eyes were very high" (meaning he stood above most boxers; figure 22). And some criticized him to me. I made no bones about bringing it to him; he never once failed to demolish the criticism. One example will serve to illustrate the finality of his argument. I told Cheng that some criticized his postures because of his bent elbow; it was more correct, they said, to have less bend and to use energy from the shoulder. He replied that reliance on the shoulder is a mark of forceful strength, *li*, rather than tenacious energy, *ching*. I said critics insisted that bending the elbow stops the ch'i. He said no, ch'i comes from the sinews, not the bones.

His advocacy of principle over rigid adherence to a set form recalls an old story. A dervish one day walked meditating by a river. From an island he heard the dervish call done incorrectly "U Ya Hu" instead of "Ya Hu." Intending to correct the caller, he got into a boat and went to the island from which the sound came. There he politely told the island dervish the correct form and was thanked. The first dervish then got into his boat and made for shore, happy that he had helped. After all, it was said that one who could repeat the formula correctly could walk on water, something, alas, that he could not yet do. His thoughts were broken by the faltering sound of the island dervish, "U Ya . . ." While the first dervish rowed on musing on the perversity and error of man, he was astounded to see the island dervish coming hastily toward him, walking on the sur⁄face of the water. The first dervish stopped rowing. The island der⁄vish walked up to him and said, "Brother, I am sorry to trouble you, but I have to ask you to repeat the correct formula, for I have trouble remembering it."

Often, when practice had concluded and we were sitting drinking tea, he could be drawn out on sundry matters and would tell of boxers he had known. He once said that boxing on the mainland had deteriorated and that Chang Chih⁄kang, one of his students, was probably the most skilled T'ai⁄chi master there.

I told him at one of these sessions that a drunk has perfect relaxa⁄tion. Was this what we were to seek? For, if it was, it would be easier to uncork wine bottles than to undergo the rigorous T'ai⁄chi discipline. "No," he said, "we do not seek this state. For the drunk gains relaxation but sacrifices his *i* ['mind,' 'intent'] to the drink."

I once was presumptuous enough to warn him against dirty tactics. He nodded. He knew. What would he do, I asked, if a wrestler grabbed hold of him; certainly this would throw the odds the other way. He acknowledged this. In the days he took on all comers, he said, he advertised that if the attacker attempted to grab him rather than to merely strike or kick him, he would forego the push and use tien⁄hsueh. Signaling me to try, he stood smiling. I tried to get hold of his jacket, and I was safe as long as I missed, but each time my fingers began to close on cloth he would touch me. When I tried to tackle him, again I felt his fingers, divorced from energy temporarily, but making their point effectively.

I learned that the unremitting practice of T'ai⁄chi is as rigorous in its way as that experienced by a Peking opera trainee, whose spartan regime begins at the age of five. The small tyke sleeps in a basket proportional to his size—but always small, inhibiting, and uncom⁄

fortable—until he is fifteen. Then the novice sleeps on a bench twelve inches wide; if he does not breathe correctly, he rolls off (the restrict✦ ed environment also figures in semen retention, without which the nurturing of ch'i is difficult).[9]

And the stories he told! When Yang Ch'eng✦fu was in Hang✦ chou, a boxer kept pestering him for a fight. Yang could not dis✦ suade him. One morning Yang was sitting on his bed, and the boxer approached with the same old suggestion. Yang gave in. "You win, come ahead." The man, a decent sort, asked him to get up from the bed. Yang said no, he would sit, but the man should attack anyhow. The man rushed in and was thrown into another bedstead, capsizing it.

Yang controlled his ch'i to such an extent that it went beyond technique. For him energy was an eternal delight. In pushing hands he could magnetize or attract your arm so that it stuck to his upper arm as it circled.

Cheng also told me of Chu Min✦i, brother✦in✦law of the Japanese puppet Wang Ching✦wei. Chu actually served as puppet ambas✦ sador to Japan after the war began in 1937. A T'ai✦chi student of Wu Chien✦ch'uan, Chu was a flamboyant exponent of the art, who gave many demonstrations, and his movements were big and flowery ("It's clever, but is it art?"). Chu was an eccentric (which is not altogether a bad thing), as is seen in the title of the doctoral thesis he wrote while studying medicine in Paris: "A Study of the Vaginal Vibrations of the Female Rabbit."

Always we would revert to the Yangs. Some of the stories of this tribe smacked strongly of the apocryphal. Old Yang Pan✦hou once accepted a challenge from a young Shao✦lin boxer. Yang side✦ stepped the impetuous one's first rush, causing him to bite the dust. The man stood up and insisted on another try. Yang turned to his young son who was watching and said, "Now you will hear the swallow sing." Then, as the attacker closed, Yang inserted his two fingers into the man's windpipe. The boxer forthwith made a sound like a swallow singing and expired.

But enough! A Sufi mystic says that when God is well disposed to His servant, He opens the gates of deeds for him and closes the gates of discussion. Cheng always emphasized that T'ai-chi is to live and practice, not to theorize about. We in America are fortunate that this great master came to live among us eight years ago. He now resides and teaches this fascinating art in New York City.

5. Master of Relaxation

*Man has no innate pugnacity. The one innate
characteristic he has is teachability.*

WESTON LABARRE

There are many T'ai-chi teachers in Taiwan and Hong Kong,
but there are only a few experts. Many do it with such skill that it is
difficult to explain why they do it badly. Until it is demonstrated,
one does not realize the great difference that exists between the merely
competent amateur and the expert professional. Wang Yen-nien
was indeed an expert professional in T'ai-chi, standing second only
to Cheng Man-ch'ing in Taiwan. Liang Tung-tsai's idea was for
me to learn rootedness for one year from Wang, then spend two years
learning the finishing flourishes from Cheng. But Wang's instruction was so valuable that I continued with him throughout the three
years, even after I had moved up to Cheng.

Weighing about 180 pounds and in his late forties, Wang was the
picture of health. He had been a colonel in World War II and had
been decorated for valor against the Japanese. He taught outside the
Grand Hotel on Round Mountain each morning, and was employed full time by several industrial firms to teach their employees
T'ai-chi. He worked himself hard—and me, also. For the first year
we averaged six hours weekly of private instruction; for the last two
we averaged even more in a group environment. My legs constantly
ached from the exertion, the lungs protested, and my body drowned
in its sweat. (Later Cheng admonished me against overexertion
leading to sweating, but at this point a framework had to be estab-
lished, work had to be done. The result was sweat). The solace was

47

in learning a great art from a fine teacher. Michel Fokine (in *Memoirs of a Ballet Master*) wrote of his training in terms reminiscent of my feelings at that time.

> How sacred these lessons were to us! What a wondrous atmosphere of respect for the accumulated richness of art ruled this small group of enthusiasts. How far removed all this was from what is happening now, when dancing is taught by people who have never even found time to study, nor have tried to dance themselves, who know nothing about the dance and—avoiding the serious approach to this complicated and difficult art—create their own 'new' forms!

Superb in contortionistic calisthenics, Wang would stand on a line and defy me to push him off. Such was his yielding ability that it was impossible. Another trick of his, done to show his rooting ability, was to put his breath in his tant'ien and let me push against his stomach. Even here, he was able to neutralize one's energy with his abdomen alone. Then we would reverse roles and he would put his hand on my abdomen. I would attempt to neutralize his push by relaxing and rooting while firming the tant'ien, but with his sensitive fingers detecting my energy I was easy for him to topple.

Wang taught me that in moving forward the toes touch down after the heel and are put down pointing straight ahead. This provides precision for the strike if it occurs at this point. But if the progression is beyond a single step you must toe out before proceeding or lose your balance. K. C. Wu (in *The Lane of Eternal Stability*) tells how a gentleman (not a fighter, remember) does it:

> See? Do not point your toes straight forward. You must point them thirty or forty degrees outward like this. The Chinese character 'eight [八].' Please put your heel down first, and allow the toes to fall gradually. See? It gives you a willowy, contemplative and unhurried air . . .

He also taught me that it is better to block from in to out rather

than the reverse or downward. This leaves you frontal to an oppo✓
nent and reflects confidence in your ability to absorb and neutralize
his efforts. I had always favored going outside an opponent's arms
and blocking inward, but he felt that the attacker could get a pur✓
chase on you even in this outside position. *Block*, however, is the
wrong word. Rather than blocking, his arms were always lightly
absorbing or detecting, like an antenna. His pushing theory was to
put his arms out; you were safe as long as you did not come within
this area. If you did, he would push you out.

Coming out of this internal system was an astounding, paradoxi✓
cal thing. Whereas contraction and tension occur automatically in
frightening or dangerous situations and a person need only control
the extent of the reaction, Wang advised that it is better if relaxation
is sustained through these moments. If attacked, a relaxed person
moves more quickly, he said. Manifestly, this relaxation has to be a
matter of degree; it is never complete. The muscles must have tonus
to survive. And muscular relaxation can be achieved only by me✓
thodical exercise, preeminently as in T'ai✓chi (figures 23–34).

This is not exclusively an Asian idea. F. J. Buytendijk (in *Pain*)
stated that methodical exercise is the only way to arrive at the desired
active relaxation. He cites the work of Edmund Jacobson and
Johannes H. Schultz on systematic muscle relaxation. (The latter's,
particularly, is of considerable value. Called *autogenics*, its current
key figure is Dr. Wolfgang Luthe of Montreal. As a technique
merging mind and body I rate it considerably higher than the

23–34. Wang Yen✓nien: relaxation exercises of T'ai✓chi

methods of the current saviors of the encounter groups, Lowen, W. Reich, and I. Rolf.) Buytendijk states that the sensation of pain is possible only when there is an involuntary "tendency to resist" within one. By asserting through relaxation dominance over the psychic center (for which read tan⁄t'ien), which is the seat of in⁄voluntary awareness, the will is able to do what the mind formerly could not; it can influence the tendency to resist to such an extent that the sensation of pain is not felt. Thus relaxation causes pain to disappear. Medical work on this problem in the United States supports this contention. Dr. Kenneth Gaarder, the psychiatrist, has stated that out of all the complexity involved in researching this sphere, one unvarying fact has emerged: deep muscle relaxation is incompatible with anxiety.

Wang taught me about holding strength on top of the head. Actually there is no strength there—only spirit. The Chinese call this "uncatchable spirit on top." This idea is the same as that where the student imagines his head suspended by a string from above, or that the head supports a book. This is a key concept in Wang's T'ai-chi. Another is that the chest is held slightly concave and the back slightly convex. Still another is that the waist must be relaxed, not stiff.

Coordination is all-important. The upper and the lower body must be integrated. The same applies to coordination between the internal and external. This can be done by calm practice of Tai-chi, in which the physique and the spirit merge and are permeated by the ch'i. The internal pertains to the spirit, an abstract thing but one that demonstrably can affect the nervous system and the entire internal physical environment. The external refers to the four limbs and other body organs. The internal and the external must go hand in hand; this is only possible with a quiet mind. Even when you stop action, your mind goes on. Wherever your mind focuses, your ch'i goes. The ch'i and the blood circulation follow the command of the mind.

The value of the spirit is enormous. My Chinese tutor, Edward E. E. Chuang (the finest gentleman I have ever met), once told me of a friend of his and the role that T'ai-chi played in his life. His friend was bedridden, nearly paralyzed, and given up for lost. An associate suggested that a T'ai-chi teacher come and do the exercise in the bedroom; it might do some good. A teacher came and did the exercise daily while the invalid looked on. Within a week there was a noticeable change in his condition; in a month the man could sit up. The sessions continued, with the patient now able to participate more physically. In three months he returned to work. The doctors attending were amazed but were unanimous in attributing the miraculous recovery to T'ai-chi. If true—and my source is impeccable—the incident is empirical evidence that the mind and spirit are as important in T'ai-chi as the body. The sick man, unable to move, absorbed what he saw and vicariously put himself into the form of the teacher doing the exercises. The benefits accruing to the teacher from doing the exercise came also to the patient, with the result that he recovered fully.

In *The Way of Chinese Painting* Sze Mai-mai states it succinctly:

> The key phrase is ch'i-yun, '*ch'i* in movement.' Translated as 'rhythmical vitality,' this is at best only partial. Rhythm is only one aspect of the total action of the *ch'i*. We can sense its meaning without difficulty but no simple definition can cover it. The fact that it has to be grasped through intuition indicates that an intellectual definition falls far short. Perhaps 'breath' is the best translation if one remembers the ancient concept of breath as soul and spirit. The Sanskrit *prana*, the Greek *pneuma*, and Latin *spiritus* have the same import as *ch'i*, likewise *ruakh* in Biblical Hebrew and the term *nefesh*, described in the Zohar as the breath and substance of the Fourth Sphere, the world of physical existence.

The Western mind is put off by this, but it need not be. Georges Braque, the modern French artist, on his seventieth birthday, said, "There is only one thing in art that is worthwhile. It is that which cannot be explained."

Wang claimed to have learned T'ai-chi from the famed Chang Ch'ing-ling on the mainland. His postures were much more bent and more acrobatic than Cheng's style. They reportedly came from the training given Chang by the Taoist Dzou, who had defeated him. (See page 38.) Chang thenceforth modified the method taught by the Yang family, bringing it closer to Dzou's teaching. And Wang's method was the long one, taking nearly fifteen minutes to complete. Besides the postures proper, he had a full range of exercises for relaxing and breathing. After coming to Taiwan, Wang also practiced frequently with Cheng Man-ch'ing. Several times I saw these two top men in the T'ai-chi world pushing hands. It is no discredit to Wang to say that Cheng toyed with him each time; it simply means that there are gradations even of high excellence.

Early morning T'ai-chi at Round Mountain was a lovely and

unforgettable experience. Several times a week I would beat the sun up, arriving there before 6 A.M. Initially it was a chore. As Napoleon once said, the rarest courage of all is the courage of early morning. But only at first. Soon growth took hold and it became a delight. On any given morning nearly one hundred persons assembled there, most of whom paid a monthly fee to Wang Yen√nien. There were obese affluent types, men and women, trying to undo years of high√ on√the√hog living. There were artisans, businessmen, boxers, and a few teen√agers and youngsters. We all followed Wang in his long version of the Yang T'ai√chi. As we continued, the sun would come up, shedding its rays on us and the city below. The two√hour train√ ing never varied: we always did the postures, pushing hands, ta√lu, and sword work, but I skipped the latter and continued pushing hands with Wang and his eager senior students (figures 35–41). But it was never boring. The variety was inside the exercise (some√ times I had the feeling that, Zenlike, the exercise was doing us). If on quitting the mountain at 8 A.M. we were not better persons than when we started, the fault lay with us and not with T'ai√chi or Wang Yen√nien.

Three times a week I would go to a rich merchant's house (one son was an avid T'ai√chi player) for a practice session with Wang. This was all pushing hands, and visiting firemen came in to try conclusions with the American. At first most pushed me easily, but over time I progressed to where I could hold my own. One learned a great deal about a man's personality by how well he stood before

35–41. Wang countering an attack

the wall. If he resisted the push by stiffening (a microcosm of life), he might blunt an attack—but only at first. Soon his rigid posture would be his undoing. If, however, a man took his uprooting graciously and came back to the fray with a smile and light arms, one knew that in time he would be a tough antagonist. It invariably worked this way. I met many men of all types, but I never met one who tried to injure me. (This was in contrast to judo. In 1948 in Chicago I was a lowly brown belt fed to a visiting *sandan* from California. Not only did this terror toss me repeatedly with *tai-otoshi*, but each time he would gratuitously throw his full weight on my prone body. Exhilarating. By the time I staggered off, John Osako and his black belts had sized the bird up, and forthwith proceeded to show our guest that there are gradations to terror.)

After an evening with Wang, despite my weariness, I would return home late in a condition that the Spanish call "joyous," but for quite another reason. I had spent an intoxicating evening, learning in the company of fine friends.

6. A Policeman's Pa=kua

Freedom is primarily the acquisition of power;
to be more exact, it is a power which is not
used.   JEAN GRENIER

In *Pa-kua*, I wrote at length on the teaching of Paul Kuo. This was of course mainly about Pa-kua, but Kuo also taught me the rudiments of orthodox Hsing-i. I often saw him practicing in a se-cluded part of Grass Mountain in the early morning and I sought him out. He began by putting me off for a year, and two years later when I was departing Taiwan ended by saying he regretted deeply that he had made me wait.

Skilled in the internal, it was Kuo who really got across to me the conceptual framework of the internal and how important were the mind (*i*) and the intrinsic energy (*ch'i*), and how unimportant the strength (*li*). A big handsome policeman, he never used strength, preferring rather to use quick brisk movements (figures 42–44). He

42–44. Paul Kuo practicing a key internal boxing technique: rise-drill-fall-overturn

believed that actual fight techniques were worthless and that it was far better to be empty of this mind clutter, so that one could respond correctly to an attack. All the while, from three other teachers, I was literally stealing one hundred tactical forms of Pa⁄kua, Kuo's specialty.

He did not believe in these set forms, as I said, and instead "walked the circle" doing the classic single and double change, all the time concentrating, relaxing, and feeling. The nimbleness with which he practiced exemplified the words of Martha Graham, the famous dancer: "There is a vitality, a life force, an energy, a quickening which is translated through you into action, and because there is only one of you in all time, this expression is unique. And if you block it, it will never exist through any other medium and it will be lost. The world will not have it."

There was no place in the practice for power: it came out of but did not go into the practice. One must be natural and avoid moving with contracted muscles. If done naturally, the field would be given over to feeling. In Tientsin, Kuo said, he and a colleague would circle blindfolded for hours and when one would say "Let's stop now" in his mind, the other would hear the message and stop.

Undogmatic, Kuo felt that it was a poor teacher who would not want his student to modify and improve a system. He himself had created two forms for beginners in Pa⁄kua. One was to breathe quietly and relax the entire body, then tremble like a horse (he was rediscovering the vibratory energy taught in T'ai⁄chi and at the Shao⁄lin Temple in Honan). The other modification he developed was a free Pa⁄kua style, with no preconceived form.

Many of the things this big and straight teacher—erect as a column of smoke, his neck rising proudly like a tower—said applied to all the internal methods. For example, the first thing you will notice after practicing an internal method for a time is that your posture and movement will be more stable, you will not wobble. Next you will feel ch'i in your arms. Finally, you will sink; your strength will leave the upper and go to the lower torso. For a while your lower back will be stiff, but the stiffness will depart suddenly, leaving you supple. Did this three-part sequence take twenty years? No, said Kuo, it could be done in three months. Old teachers would never concede this, insisting instead on two decades.

Kuo told me of Shang Yun-hsiang, he of the potbelly who studied under Li Ts'un-i on the mainland. Shang was illiterate and poor, so poor that daily he walked barefoot twenty miles to and from his home, doing all the while the bamboo style (a half-step) *peng ch'uan* of Hsing-i, his shoes slung around his neck. For this he was called "iron-foot." Kuo said that his fingers were like spikes: he could penetrate a leather belt and grab a rib, and would let a man stand on his abdomen and would bounce him off. Kuo told me also of Wang Hsiang-chai, famed but not liked in Hopei. Wang loved to fight and lost only to Shang Yun-hsiang. His method consisted entirely of circles; every block was an attack.

Kuo could do Hsing-i at least four different ways including one going backward. He had been taught well by Chang Hung-ch'ing and Kuo Han-chih in Tientsin, men never known to have laughed nor to have lost a fight.

We met three times weekly for two years, and it was rigorous work. Kuo taught no one else. He believed that a student should earn the right to have a teacher, and to keep one. I nearly lost him at one juncture. One afternoon, forgetting that he was coming, I was practicing a Shao-lin grasping exercise of throwing a thirty-pound piece of concrete into the air and catching it. He approached me and sauntered by and into the house without a word. I sensed my error and hastened in. He quickly pointed out that such "hard" exercises not only opposed the principles of the internal system but that they would also impede my progress. If I continued, he said, he would be forced to discontinue the instruction.

Kuo always stressed celerity and crispness and believed that in practice one should appear like a lady dancing, and in a fight, like a tiger (figure 45). After learning these forms and with diligent practice (Kuo, a Christian who really worked at it would say that

45. *Kuo in Hsing-i posture*

the Devil is diligent; so ought we to be) one reached the ultimate: to respond instantly without thought of threat. Breathing should be done so that the strike is made on exhalation but the stomach is hardened (the muscles contracted) at the same time. Similar to Minnesota Fats's advice on billiards ("The tip of your nose should be in a straight line with the cue and the cue ball"), Kuo said that the fist should be lined up with your nose and your opponent.

Had he ever been forced to use his boxing? In the best way, he said. When I questioned "the best," he dilated. As a policeman he had been caught several times in near-riot situations. But each time the crisis crumbled as he walked into the middle of the miscreants. He believed that the boxing spoke through him, that he exuded the spirit, and that the troublemakers sensed it and were deterred. The best course always, he said, is to neutralize a situation without recourse to the physical: this is truly the Taoist way.

When I went to say good-by he was genuinely sorry. I told him what I would my other teachers: I had only scratched the surface (*p'i mao*; literally "skin" and "hair," meaning superficial) in my study. He replied (echoing Erasmus), "In great things, it is enough to have tried." I responded that for me this was not enough, that I wanted to master the art, and that now this goal was made doubly difficult of achievement by my returning to America where there were no teachers. He acknowledged this but remonstrated that by definition what was difficult was not impossible. By the very nature of the *nei-chia*, it is not what comes out of it but what goes into it—that is, into the person practicing it. By extension this smacked of the Buddhist saying: "An inch of meditation, an inch of Buddha." And with this encouragement, I left this splendid man.

7. Bone=locker Extraordinary

As long as the soul stands erect it holds the body high and does not allow the years to touch it. NIKOS KAZANTZAKIS

Han Ch'ing⁄t'ang is a famous mainland Shao⁄lin master and the best *ch'in⁄na* (the art of seizing) artist in Southeast Asia. I met him through Liang Tung⁄tsai. The latter had spoken casually one day of his master in ch'in⁄na. I immediately asked to meet the man and Liang obliged. Han was cordial, and when I asked for instruction he complied immediately without ceremony. For two years we met for an hour and a half every Sunday (figures 46–47). He was a good mentor, and the wine he imbibed on his way to our practice place, while a bit wild for the discriminating nose, did nothing to his stable bone locks.

Ch'in⁄na is an integral part of most boxing systems as well as of wrestling. But it is also a specialization, an art unto itself. It was originally called the "art of splitting sinews and twisting bones" and, also, "pinching and grasping to unearth a person." It includes some wrestling and striking techniques. It uses both soft and hard methods

46–47. Han Ch'ing⁄t'ang counters by scooping

in those situations Han described as " . . . hand to hand—there is no place to go," quoting an old saying. Because it involves superb control, Han believed it superior to striking and kicking methods and ideal for police work. The masters of it were few, but their skill was of an extremely high order. I learned some ch'in-na from Hung I-hsiang, Yuan Tao, Liao Wu-ch'ang, and Wu Ti-p'en, but the best skill clearly resided in Han, he of the jocular eyes and the irritatingly long fingernails.

Our routine was, first off, to learn the nine basic movements of ch'in-na, which, incidentally, are illustrated in his book on the subject, *Ching-ch'a Ying-yung Chi-neng* (Techniques for Police Use; unfortunately, it has not been translated into English). These bone locks are most scientific, and I believe superior to the Japanese and American versions. Once learned, they were modified to allow one to respond to any counter movement an opponent might make. Ch'in-na is light on theory, heavy on practice. A thorough knowledge of anatomy is necessary, as is the will to endure the long hours of effort required. The best arm to attack, Han felt, is the weaker, the left. Each tactic initially unbalances the opponent before effecting the lock.

Strangling and even some strikes were included in the ch'in-na curriculum. Han was an acknowledged Shao-lin boxer and weapons expert, and his teaching in these fields was first-rate. In fact, ch'in-na is a specialization taken only after the student has gained proficiency in boxing (figures 48–49).

"Your judo," he said, "teaches you to throw your opponent, but

48–49. Han counters with scissors plus

often this is dangerous since the opponent then has his feet free. Many 'dog' boxers would ride the throw and then kick the thrower. If the man is immobilized standing, he has no freedom to retaliate."

And again: "Most karate started from spillage from Fukien Prov-ince. It is in no sense profound. The flat fist that it delights in is too short and too vulnerable to locks. The standing fist is far superior. When your target is a bony area, use a speedy retracting punch; when it is a soft part, use a heavier punch and do not retract it."

Some other fighting tactics he taught: When an opponent tries a two-finger poke at your eyes, use two fingers, insert, and fold back breaking one of his fingers. On a frontal choke, unbalance harshly forward before applying, thus preventing him from attacking your groin. He even showed me a novel way of committing suicide by choking (infinitely more subtle than the method used by an English-man of strapping himself over the mouth of a cannon and igniting the charge), which he maintained some boxers on the mainland ha⁻ used. Clasping hands on the back of the head the thumbs bring pressure on the carotids and hold it while a count to thirty is made. He insisted that the pressure can be maintained, but I believe that unconsciousness would ensue, the pressure would stop, and one would come around in a minute or so. However, I did not try it, nor do I advise the reader to. Han also was adept at striking; one of his favorites was to fake a wide right hook at an opponent's head and then change it into a straight knifing thrust to the side of the throat when the opponent blocks in anticipation of the hook.

Han was so adept that he is the only man I have seen who could do that which is the crux of the seizing arts: capture a hand while it is striking. Also, I had not thought anyone could improve on the *shime* ("strangle") arts of the Japanese, but his chokes I found to be technically more effective. On frontal chokes he would jerk you forward and choke while imprisoning your leg at the same time. On *hadaka-jime* where the Japanese stress the push of the left hand, he used it only to support the right hand, which knifes into the carotid artery.

I was not always so lucky in my teachers. I was once taken to the home of another famed Shantung boxer, who was then seventy⁄four and who had started boxing at twelve. I plied him with gifts and helped rebuild the hovel he lived in. He finally agreed to teach me. For a month I worked with his students at performing chains of ch'in⁄na, and all the while the old man, whose triceps hung from his arms like sacks, sat on a chair and said four things.

1. It is best to avoid blocking. Dodge and strike.
2. Striking is better than ch'in⁄na unless the ch'in⁄na man is expert.
3. The flat fist is no good.
4. Skill consists of little things.

When it became apparent that we had no rapport and that besides gouging me financially, he was not going to release any of the essence of his art, I quit going.

8. The Wrestling Champion

. . . the subtle rapture of a postponed power.
OLIVER W. HOLMES

Shang Tung-sheng was the most disciplined boxer I met. I never saw him smile and I seldom heard him speak. Severe, the product of a spartan existence (a Moslem, he neither smoked nor used spirits), he asked for no favors and gave none. At our first meeting he began things by slapping me significantly (that is, sharply but not too heavily) in the groin. This served to establish the lines of our relationship.

Chou Ch'i-ch'un had introduced me to Shang. And through him I arranged a one-and-one-half-hour training session each week at the Police Officers' Training College, where Shang taught traditional Chinese wrestling (*shuai chiao*) and other fighting forms. Shang had won the heavyweight wrestling championship of the mainland in 1935, although he weighed only 160 pounds at the time. He told me that his closest friend was entered in the middleweight class (160–80 pounds), so Shang entered the heavier category. Both won.

He set about teaching me traditional Chinese wrestling. His method was to use senior students to illustrate the throws and to fall for me as I learned them. Before long I found myself somewhat of a guinea pig for traditional wrestlers from all over the island. They came in all shapes and sizes. Few, however, had any real wrestling ability. Even using their rules (no ground work, chokes, or locks) I invariably defeated them. Only once was I bested. It was the night Wang Shu-chin came to watch.

Shang instructed me to use only the shuai chiao techniques he had taught me, and no judo, in a match with his best student. He was obviously intent on showing Wang how well his wrestling stacked up with that of the American. He put me at a distinct dis- advantage, but I went ahead with it. In the early phases of the match, overconcerned with using only his stuff, I was taken over with a shoulder technique. Behind, I tried to catch up, but was unable to with shuai chiao against an overly defensive opponent. Finally, forgetting his restriction, I swept the wrestler onto his back (shuai chiao is defective in that sweeps are not in its repertoire). Shang was even more silent than usual after the tie.

The wrestling itself is a standing form, quite rigid, and can be characterized as early (1880) jujutsu without the ground work. On the mainland it can be traced back to at least 700 B.C., when it ranked with archery and horsemanship as a martial art.[1] In the Ming dynasty (1368–1644) a profusely illustrated book on it, *Wan Pao Ch'uan Shu* (The Precious and Complete Book), was published and transmitted to Japan, where it aroused such interest that Chinese wrestling teachers were invited to Japan. The postures are similar to judo, so much so that I believe that judo developed from shuai chiao rather than from an indigenous Japanese source. In his home Shang had a huge drawing over one hundred years old of the basic shuai chiao throws. I studied it several times (he would not permit me to photograph it), and the similarities with modern judo tech- niques were striking. One could see there early *uchimata*, *haraigoshi*, *ouchigari*, and other techniques. Although it may have fathered judo, shuai chiao has failed to evolve and keep pace with it.

On Taiwan, shuai chiao had taken a poor second place to judo, which became entrenched during the long Japanese rule over the island. As far as I know, it is not practiced at all in Southeast Asia. Shang lamented that the Nationalist government did little to pro- mote it, but I believe that shuai chiao lost out simply because it had not evolved. This is not to say, however, that if you put top judoka into the coarse, tight jackets of shuai chiao and made them fight within the Chinese regulations that they would win. And it certainly does not mean that Shang himself could not operate successfully in a match with a quality judoka, each using his own method and rules. He was that rough. On the mainland he had once defeated a Mon-golian champion by clouting him with his elbow. And in Peking, he said, he had competed with many Japanese judoka and was never beaten.

Once we were driving slowly down a poorly lighted street in a heavy rain, and a pedestrian berated me for coming too close to him. Not understanding his guttural speech, I took it in good form. But the man, quite the most ugly I can ever remember, continued his tongue lashing. Shang motioned me to stop, got out, and said some-thing too quietly for me to hear. The man disappeared quickly. I asked Chou what Shang had said to the man. "It is best that you hurry on" was his translation.

Shang's self-defense was first-rate. He liked the open hand and advised that one should hit first, then grapple, not vice versa. Like Cheng Man-ch'ing, he cautioned against using full power in any technique; to thwart counters some power should always be re-served. Also, he exemplified the highest shuai chiao ability: whether in wrestling or self-defense the opponent is locked and often has to accept the throw itself to escape the consequences of a lock. But even the escape is none too easy. On the mainland they wrestled on dirt, and falls were apt to be traumatic. This forced the wrestlers to fall on their sides, slightly curled, while cuddling the head with both hands. They thus eschewed the break-fall of judo, and I cannot but believe that they were worse off for it.

I once submitted to Hung Hsien-mieng's offer to pick me up, to "show me something" (he was drunk, but I learned much from drunks). Predictably when he got me up he tripped, and I fell onto the concrete of the upper room of the brothel we were practicing in. I used the judo *ukemi*, rather than that of shuai chiao, striking the concrete smartly with my arm as I dropped. The bone I sheared in my elbow was a small price, I felt, for the consequences I would have encountered had I protected only my head and left my body to the harshness of the concrete.

Shang often was rough with me, but I minded not, practicing always with the hope that he would go beyond the rudimentary. He never did, but it was partly my fault. He wanted me to give up boxing and practice nothing but shuai chiao. I refused, saying that at my age and in the time available I thought it best to probe the entire body of *ch'uan fa*, not just the wrestling. Finally, a year after we began, he relayed through Chou the word that I had had it, he no longer had the time to teach me. I drew Chou out. Shang had seen a photograph in a Hong Kong magazine of me with Cheng Man-ch'ing. Sharing me with a boxer at odds with the entire boxing community was too much for him. This ended our association, and, though I learned something from him, I sometimes have speculated what would have happened had I gone along with him. I usually end by concluding that my choice was the proper one.

9. Other Teachers

Tzu-ch'i of Nan-po asked Ju Yi: 'You are old but your complexion is like a child. Why?' 'I have been taught a method.'

CHUANG TZU

Besides the principal teachers cited above, many other boxers taught me. Unfortunately, I was unable to practice regularly enough for a long enough period to claim sustained instruction from them. But because they were all ingredients in the story and deserve mention, I dilate on them below.

CH'EN P'AN-LING

Until his death at seventy-seven in 1967, Ch'en P'an-ling was without doubt more knowledgeable on the principles, rationale, and practice of Chinese boxing than anyone in the world. He was one of the few fighters in Taiwan who was famed earlier on the mainland. His father had undergone the severe training at the Shao-lin Temple in Honan Province and had selected the finest teachers for his son. Although well educated and well connected (a hydraulic engineer, he had been chairman of the Honan Province Kuomin-tang headquarters since 1944), his first love was boxing. He even studied T'ai-chi at the famed Honan village of Ch'en Chia K'ou. Ch'en rose so high in boxing ranks that he supervised several of the provincial fistic tournaments before World War II in Honan, one of the prime boxing provinces on the mainland. During World

War II he was made deputy chief of the Central Boxing Association at Chungking, where he also headed a commission to collect,
edit, and publish material on fifty-five forms of *wu-shu* (unfortunately, most of the material was lost when the Communists took
over the mainland).

When I knew him Ch'en was president of a college at Taichung
and the highly respected head of the Chinese Boxing Association
in Taiwan. (See figure 1.) In his twilight years he had lost some of
his youthful ability, but still, watching him go through his "syn-
thetic" boxing, one knew that here was one of a better breed, a champion fighter. He told me once that he had practiced staff work under
a famed ninety-year-old master in Peking. During a go at conclusions
young Ch'en was able not only to deflect the stick of the master but,
in the same movement, to cause the oldster to lose his weapon. Many
students laughed at this. The master repossessed his weapon and told
the class not to laugh, that this was an occasion of seriousness. "Why
do you laugh?" he asked. "This was a splendid movement showing
that young Ch'en has achieved a breakthrough in technique. No
real teacher begrudges a point scored by a student. It only reflects
well on the teacher. I teach all of you to first overcome me, then
yourselves. Yet only Ch'en shows some ability—but only toward the
first objective. The rest of you laugh. Rather than laugh, work! But
for now all of you except Ch'en leave."

General Yang Tsung-ting, a close associate of Ch'en, told me that
as a student Ch'en did not follow the rules of protocol, refused to
kowtow, and was regarded as a radical on this account. This carried
over to his teaching; he charged no one nor did he insist on ritual.
But he was selective in whom he taught.

Yang had also researched *wu-shu*, although not as assiduously as
Chou Ch'i-ch'un (see page 84). It may be well to give some of
Yang's views on it. In the old days boxing was necessary for self-
defense. During the Sung dynasty (960–1279) the Shao-lin temples
gathered and modified the existing boxing skills. (Although *Shao-
lin Temple* commonly refers to the temple in Honan Province, there

were two, the other being in Fukien Province. A fellow officer of Yang's actually saw the Fukien temple. Chou, however, did not believe that the evidence for the Fukien temple was good enough to establish it as fact.) The third Manchu emperor, Yung Cheng (reigned 1722–35), burned down both temples. Rather than destroy-ing the Shao-lin teaching, this act only triggered its spread through-out China. Emperor Ch'ien Lung (reigned 1735–95) rebuilt the Fukien temple thirty-seven years after it was burned. The Honan temple also was rebuilt. All the great boxers studied there. The hard, soft, and tremble arts were all taught.

With the creation of the republic in 1912, communications improved and boxing spread widely. Until then boxing was on a small scale, except at the Shao-lin temples. They were like univer-sities, and graduates often created their own styles. But Shao-lin was the root. Initially, the novice was given menial jobs and with time and energy worked his way up to a higher status. But not everyone could gain entrance. (This is reminiscent of the desert saints who quit civilization in droves in the third and fourth centuries. Fourth-century Christain writers spoke of their efforts in sporting terms, recounting their feats and fasting records. Called *athletes in exile*, these monks invariably had monastery doors shut in their faces. For ten days after being admitted, no one would speak to them, and they were forced to prostrate themselves before each monk, who delighted in spitting on them. The teaching of humility takes odd forms and knows no geographic limits.)

Yang said that ch'i can be translated "energy" and is quite impor-tant. The proofs for it, however, are subjective. Everyone is born with it, but unless it is cultivated it is lost. The *hu k'ou* ("tiger's mouth," the space between the stretched thumb and index finger, used in Hsing-i and Pa-kua) permits the ch'i to come to the top of the index finger. If the digits are not stretched the ch'i cannot get across.

Yang had met Tu Hsin-wu, one of the greatest boxers of all time. Tu stood about six feet tall. Very thin, he gave no hint of being a boxer (as Saint/Simon wrote of an acquaintance, "He was a humble man, whose physiognomy promised nothing"). He could turn his head 180° and do marvelous things quite beyond even the most skilled of the rest of us. He had a queue, and when it dangled in front of his eyes in doing a form, he would take his foot as though it were his hand and move the queue.

But to get back to Ch'en: by combining the intellectual with the athletic, he demolished John P. Marquand's thought (in *Thank you, Mr. Moto*), which I found under the glass top of my desk when I first arrived in Taiwan in August, 1959: "I had learned from my years in China that undue exertion of nearly any form leads to diffi/ cult consequences, and at any rate is undignified." Even on the wrong side of seventy, this champion boxer continued his boxing and teaching until his demise.

His advice to me was always terse and profound. He said that the internal aspects (mind, ch'i, and strength) must be attuned to the external (eye, hand, and foot) if boxing is to come to full flower, but in anything less than complete coordination, it is better to rely on the internal. Pa/kua and Hsing/i must be practiced with the same relaxedness as T'ai/chi, but at a normal boxing speed. There is no greater mistake than to practice them forcefully like karate. The body must act and react as a single entity; no component acts indepen/ dently. And it must be kept open and not contracted; otherwise some components (for example, the shoulders or arms) will act to the detriment of the whole, and the action will lose trueness and suffer appreciably.

Ch'en told me this about the Shao/lin temples. Students there usually practiced three times a day, two hours at a time: in the early morning, immediately after lunch, and in the evening. For advanced students, there was also a special practice at midnight. Initially, students underwent group instruction; after reaching a certain level they were taught individually. After a student had completed his studies he had to pass through four or five gates at which his teachers attacked him. If he was successful in thwarting these attempts, the student was permitted to leave the temple as a graduate.

I worked closely with Ch'en on organizational matters of the association. During his waning years he published his own "gath_rered" method of T'ai‑chi and a book on shuai chiao. I feel sure that there are writings of his unpublished, for once he spoke of a sched‑ule involving all the major arts. I recall this because I had urged him to put out a general work covering all the arts prior to one on specific methods. He sensed my seriousness and treated me with more respect than I deserved.

His last years were spent in a depressed state. His good name besmirched in one of life's episodes in which nothing one does avails, he nonetheless was most kind to me. I was only able to appreciate it much later when I, too, encountered such an episode. I met him several times in Taipei, and each time I went to Taichung he greeted me anew, bidding his disciples to accommodate me fully. His two sons, Yun‑ch'ao and Yun‑ch'ing, are in the unenviable posi‑tion of carrying his name and fighting tradition forward. But what a glorious thing, too, to have had such a father!

WANG SHU‑CHIN

Wang Shu‑chin is the greatest exponent of Hsing‑i and Pa‑kua in Taiwan. A big Buddhalike man scaling well over 230 pounds, he frowns on the hard Shao‑lin external methods. Brick breaking and tile shattering, he said, would never prove anything until bricks and tiles began to think and move like humans.

Wang's private life was something of a mystery. Reportedly he owned several rice stores and was a leader in a religious movement. I do know he was a vegetarian and unmarried. Because he lived in Taichung, I saw him infrequently, but each time I met him he went out of his way to impart solid instruction. A student of the famed Chang Chao‑tung on the mainland, Wang's Hsing‑i and Pa‑kua were orthodox and machined to perfection. With his bulk, hands

50. Wang Shu-chin taking Hung I-hsiang's punch comfortably

the size of small rosebushes, and his surprising speed, the goal of Hsing-i—to occupy the enemy's territory—was adroitly done. The internal system stresses the cultivation of ch'i, deep breathing, and a drastically different approach to the mechanical aspects of fighting than does Shao-lin. But like Shao-lin it has many advocates who can withstand with impunity a foot or fist to the midriff (figure 50). Wang not only has this skill, but he can actually use his vast stomach against one's fist on impact so as to produce a broken wrist. Throughout Asia he has been tested, and no one comes close to hurting him. Leading Japanese karate masters have bowed to him after failing on his paunch.

But this alone cannot make a fighter. Frank "Cannonball" Rich-ards, the carnival performer, and various other "marshmallow gut" types in the United States have the capability to take a stomach attack. Indeed, Harry Houdini died as a result of his inability with this feat. After ineffectually punching Wang's belly once, I asked if he could take a solar plexus strike. "Try it," he said. I did—several times, with no effect. But beyond this special skill Wang could do something beyond the ability of all the fighters I saw. He could take any kick to the lower extremities (excluding, of course, the groin). I kicked him repeatedly on his knee, calf, and ankle until my feet ached, all with no effect.

"How do you do it?" I asked.

His answer: "Ch'i."

Such skills do not connote anything more than defensive ability. Coupled in Wang, these skills left an attacker only two targets, the head and the groin, both very mobile and difficult to hit. But one still might properly ask, could he fight?

He could and did. He has spent much of his time in recent years in Japan and has fought several high-ranking karate men. No one has come close to defeating this seventy-year-old warrior. In the process he has come to a supreme depreciation of karate. He feels that the original forms borrowed from China have been distorted and that the nonsensical high kicks and vigorous body hardening avail nothing when confronted with real technique.

And technique he has. He uses the Hsing-i fist with a corkscrew twist from one inch out with more effect than most men get from a full-stance strike. John Bluming, Dutch amateur judo champion and Mas Oyama's prize foreign karateka, even though he had hurt his wrist on Wang's stomach, disparaged him to me once when I was visiting Tokyo. "What else can he do?" asked John. I took John to Wang and asked that he be shown the corkscrew, but to keep it gentle. Wang put his relaxed fingers on Bluming's stomach, curled them into a fist and screwed. Bluming bent over in agony, and has since been a believer.

The fist is but part of his arsenal. His Pa-kua palm is like iron; his fingers fall on one like drills. An unlovely trick he likes is to lure

51–53. Wang doing the heng-ch'uan of Hsing-i

one close and then pull him directly onto himself, while he bumps the unlucky one with his gut. Early on he perpetrated this tactic on me and I, too, was converted. Hung I⁄hsiang later told me that he had been knocked unconscious by the trick.

A conversation I had with him after practice one night at Shang Tung⁄sheng's house is revealing. He said that to gain *kung fu* in the fingers, iron sand as used by Shao⁄lin adepts was not really necessary. Self⁄training regularly in Hsing⁄i is all that is required (figures 51–53). Many famed boxers never used iron sand. One boxer he knew on the mainland could break a brick by slapping it, but this ability had cost him the use of his fingers; he could not pick up a coin. And this, he averred, was a real lack because the grasp in fighting is worth quite as much as the strike. Generally, open⁄hand striking is to be preferred over the fist; the fingers are longer and have more variation. The key to the Hsing⁄i *peng⁄ch'uan* standing fist is that as you hit you press down, forcing an "up⁄reaction," which facilitates uprooting. All good boxers drop their shoulders in punching. Finally, he told me that one good action is worth ten mediocre ones.

To my query about Chang Chao⁄tung, Wang replied that he had studied under Chang from 1929 to 1938. When Chang died, Wang went to Peking and studied under Hsiao Hai⁄po there and the famous Wang Hsiang⁄chai at Tientsin. Wang's students often stood five to six hours in snowy, freezing weather, their arms held up in an open embrace posture, practicing the breathing methods of Hsing⁄i. Wang Hsiang⁄chai felt so depressed by Chang's death that he changed the name of Hsing⁄i to Ta⁄ch'eng Ch'uan ("Great Achievement Boxing").

Although Wang Shu⁄chin greatly respected his later teachers, he believed that none could stand with Chang. He felt strongly that Chang was superior to other great masters such as Sun Lu⁄t'ang and Tu Hsin⁄wu. Chang's teaching was fairly typical of the great masters. At first he was gentle and watched from a chair. But if the student made repeated mistakes or was lazy, he struck him. There were many great boxers in north China during that period and,

Wang believed, Chang was the greatest. Some were publicized; others were mystery men. One such mystery master (this from a source other than Wang) was Liu Pan-hsien, an albino who lived in Tientsin. Liu never seemed to age. Skilled in the Taoist methods of retaining semen, he once went through a whole house of prostitu-tion in the foreign concession, delighting the girls while never him-self climaxing. Liu may have been one of the teachers of the famed Tu Hsin-wu.

Coming from a glorious tradition, this vast man, this vegetarian, this fine boxer continues to teach a few students in Taiwan. In recent years he has spent considerable time in Japan, teaching T'ai-chi but, significantly, not Hsing-i or Pa-kua. Phil Relnick, one of his T'ai-chi students in Tokyo during this period, told me that he and several other Americans shivered through the exercises done outdoors in the Tokyo cold. To warm themselves they would grasp Wang's hand, which conveyed heat like a radiator. One simply could not practice with Wang and disbelieve in the ch'i.

WILLIAM CH'EN

I trained under William Ch'en in Taiwan and in New York City. He fools you (figure 54). Meek, slender, and quiet, he might be a scholar or a student of the *Book of Changes*, never a boxer. But most

54. William Ch'en

assuredly he is. I saw him neutralize Wang Yen-nien quite effectively in pushing hands, and while he did not defeat Wang, neither was he defeated. He is so relaxed that he appears to have no bones.

Ch'en probably climbed higher than any of Cheng Man-ch'ing's disciples, except the converted White Crane boxer Huang Sheng-hsien (who after learning T'ai-chi moved to Singapore and ac-quired some fame there; in 1970 he publicly thrashed a "wrestler" in a bout that, on the basis of news accounts I have seen, lacks credibility). He even studied for a period at Cheng's house, where he was being treated for an illness. He was one of the few T'ai-chi adepts to enter the Taiwan annual free fighting tournament, emerg-ing as champion in the lightweight division in 1958. From Taiwan he went to Singapore, Malaysia, and Bangkok, and finally to New York City, where he now lives, carrying the T'ai-chi gospel.

As one believing and incorporating Cheng's ideas on relaxation, Ch'en stands high. He truly exemplifies the thought that humility is the deep art of the soul to relax completely. In stipulating that T'ai-chi should be done slowly, smoothly, and uninterruptedly, he cited the analogy of tea in a pot. After sufficient time and after the water achieves the proper heat, the tea leaves sink to the bottom. Without these factors (time, heat), even poking the leaves will not make them sink. Once the leaves have sunk, the pot must be handled slowly and steadily or the leaves will surface. In T'ai-chi with time and proper nurturing the ch'i will sink. Once sunk it can still rise if the body does not move slowly and steadily in the exercise and in life.

The Chinese never tire of disputatious talk on philosophy. One discovers at least a half dozen disparate theses on T'ai-chi and the ch'i. The clearest and most reasonable definition I have seen is that *t'ai-chi*, as a philosophical term, corresponds to the *Tao* of the ancient Lao-tse and Chuang Tzu school: it is the essence of the cosmos, the ultimate reality. Indeed, it translates as "Supreme Ultimate." Chou Tun-i (1017–73), going back to the ancient *Book of Changes*, fully developed *t'ai-chi* as the primary principle of all things, the cause and purpose of the evolution of the universe. Intrinsic energy, or ch'i, is simply the universal urge of the *t'ai-chi*. The Chinese believe that this life principle, which animates all nature, as it is gathered and nurtured, will make for a new man.

The exercise then is merely a microcosmic functioning of these macrocosmic forces. It renders theory into action, which Kazantzakis calls the "ultimate most holy form of theory." In proving the theory, it develops it and spreads it over everything we do; it is not a veneer but a patina that permeates.

Apropos this, Gilbert Seldes wrote some strikingly relevant words years ago, in *The Seven Lively Arts*. He recalled a theory of Remy De Gourmont in which that writer stated that if life is worth anything per se, then we err in living it in a series of high moments separated by long hours of dullness. Rather, we ought to take the amount of energy we possess and spread it as thin as possible, relishing each moment for itself, each being as good as any other. Seldes observed that living thus is like burning always with a hard gemlike flame (the idea and even the phraseology used earlier by Walter Pater in *The Renaissance*), which manifests itself in a calm but intensely aware life. Seldes went on:

> We have all had these days of halcyon perfection, when the precise degree of warmth was a miracle, when the aroma of a wine seemed to have the whole fragrance of the earth, when one could do anything or nothing and be equally content. In the presence of great works of art we experience something similar. We are suspended between the sense of release from life, the desire to die before the image of the supremely beautiful, and a new-found capacity for living. Our daily existence gives us no such opportunity; we cannot live languorously because we have no leisure, and we are compelled to be intense at rare intervals if life isn't to be entirely a hoax and a bore. In the preoccupations of daily life a tragic incident or an outburst of temper or a perfectly cut street dress or the dark-light before a storm, may give us, apart from our emotional lives, the intensity we require.

We rather defend ourselves from the impact of great beauty, of nobility, of high tragedy, because we feel ourselves incompetent to master them; we preserve our individual lives even if we diminish them.

Although Seldes probably never heard of t'ai-chi, his words (and De Gourmont's) are singularly appropriate. One has but to read Lao-tse, which is the base of t'ai-chi, to realize the remarkable similarity. But where these authors differed from Lao-tse and T'ai-chi was in not knowing that this energy is not restricted to a given amount, that it can be added to, accumulated, stored, and used in wondrous ways. T'ai-chi is the process and ch'i the medium through which this process functions so that it can be said of a man that (as Kazantzakis said of Odysseus), "He lived every moment intensely, with quality."

Ch'en's teaching was a model of quality. The student seeks a coalescence of sinking relaxation of the body and calmness of the mind, and the movements should suggest swimming in air. The three pumps of the circulatory system are constantly exercised: the legs, by the low posture; the diaphragm, by the low breathing; and the heart, by the rhythmic movements. (The teaching is Ch'en's; the felicitous phrasing is that of my T'ai-chi colleague, Ben Fusaro.) The head must be kept erect, and the body should neither rise and fall nor stop and go. The rhythm must be unhurried and sustained

55–63. Other T'ai-chi auxiliary exercises

(figures 55–63). Initially (in the Beginning posture), when you raise your arms, turn your elbows in but not too far, keep your shoulders down, and think of the top of the wrists. Enhance your root by bend/ ing your knees slightly and by contracting the upper thighs. Keep your knees turned slightly inward. Do not take too wide a step. Slump your shoulders and move as if you are very weary.

The key thing is to relax. James Stephens once asked AE (George Russell), the famed Irish writer and mystic, where he got all of his energy from. AE answered that he got it from a sinking of himself into the meditation that is known in every system as "the practice of the presence of God." From religious and philosophical writings he learned a discipline of training his mind, memory, and will, and in two years he mastered the system from which energy comes. The allusion to religion should not vex one. Some forms of Christi/

anity held, and still hold, an attachment to methods of quieting similar to those used by Asians. In the Greek Orthodox tradition, breathing was slowed and controlled, the eyes were fixated on the heart and navel, to let the mind go back into the heart, and an inner warmth and physical perception of a divine light was created. To this a layer of prayer was added. The Jesus Prayer ("Jesus Christ, son of God the Father, have mercy on me a sinner") was intoned continually until it became an intrinsic part of breathing. Saint Ignatius Loyola in the *Exercises* gave precise directions on bodily attitudes during meditation, and Vladimir Soloviev, a Russian religious writer, recommended controlled breathing as an aid to prayer. These methods then, do not differ markedly from those of the Taoists, nor does the target: God or Tao. The Taoist aimed to "still the heart" by emptying it of all distracting thought and emotion. The emptiness creates a receptivity to Tao. As Lieh Tzu states, "To a mind that is still, the whole universe surrenders."

But the stillness must be lived. To keep it in a static context may be fine for sedentary monks and yogi, but it does us little good. An old Taoist text says:

> The stillness in stillness is not the real stillness; only when there is stillness in movement does the universal rhythm manifest.

Ch'en extrapolated the stillness in the T'ai-chi postures to the pushing hands (*t'ui shou*) exercise. He insisted that relaxation must be maintained when you push with a partner. Bring your arms into play naturally. Let no more than four ounces of your opponent's energy come onto your body. Try to neutralize this without recourse to your arms. There are two times propitious for pushing: (1) When your opponent's weight is to the rear, bring your rear foot just in back of your front foot, step off with your front foot and push, and (2) as he pushes, neutralize, and as he goes backward merge with his momentum and push. Let your body do the pushing. Think of your forearms near the elbows, and actually soften your hands as you push. Insert your lead foot deeply into your opponent's posture so that when you push your knee does not go over your toes. When you push sink your ch'i to the navel and give a light, almost inau/dible *kiai* (sounding something like *huh*). As your heel hits, the entire body pushes outward, the effect aided by thinking in the direction of the push.

Ch'en's pushing technique differed markedly from Cheng Man/Ch'ing's, in that he used the two hands simultaneously as the body weight came forward and the heel of the front foot touched down. This triangulation method, in which the resultant of the two force vectors is directed at a given point, adds strength to the push. While Cheng also used the method, he was more leisurely about it, and often made extensive use of just one hand. Also, whereas Ch'en preferred to avoid the opponent's hands in order to push his body, Cheng urged direct application against the arms.

Ch'en also stressed the self/defense aspects of the art more than the master did. He could take any punch on his upper torso and would let rocks be broken on and motorcycles driven across his abdomen. His relaxed punches and kicks were extremely fast and shook the recipient to the core. In New York City he was attacked by a local boxer, and the miscreant required extensive medical treatment as a result, the onlookers claiming never to have seen the counters that undid that worthy. Cheng's approach was quite different: you learned the combative aspects after you had mastered the therapeutic discipline. And Cheng did not teach the function of the postures per se; he believed that if the T'ai/chi body is developed, any attack could be neutralized and countered without recourse to a specific riposte for a specific attack. Inevitably, the difference in approach brought a strain in their relationship.

Ch'en told me a story of the famed Yang Lu/ch'an that illu/strates their difference on the use of the postures. Once Yang visited a small village and was scorned because he did not look like a boxer. The town's best battler was brought in, and he told Yang to prepare himself. Without taking a stance, Yang replied that he was ready. The man attacked and was killed on the spot by a hand (from the

Beginning posture) that no one saw. Ch'en said the story was told him by Cheng. But the master disavowed authorship; in fact, he said that this posture is not really meant for use in this way. The hands are raised to circulate the ch'i, nothing more. Probably nei⁄ ther is wrong. The posture may be used in this way, but one should not train as if this were the goal. If one does, the ch'i is subverted and we end with a mere mechanical counter. If the ch'i flows, then it may well be that when attacked one responds with this measure but the response is done spontaneously through the ch'i, not the thinking brain.

William Ch'en would say leave all to the ch'i. Paradoxically, this idea, the epitome of T'ai⁄chi, is nowhere better expressed than by Constantin Brunner, a famous German philosopher (in *Science, Spirit, Superstition*).

With a transformed mind now will you think of what is in store for you: that the storm and whirlwind of motion will come and tear you along towards new existences. *Omnia diversis gradibus animate*—you are at one with all this. All is truly one in the one dance of motion. This is why all things act upon each other and pass into each other. And that is why all passes into you and your animateness, just as you pass into all: because all is animated with inner thinking. If you find and realize yourself as part of the entirety of this motion of nature then you grasp nature at the root of her deepest inwardness. It is you who both fulfil and reveal the law of motion in your thinking.

Brunner ends his book as follows:

We renounce the *Gusto celeste*, we dream no dreams of the sweetest and loveliest of becalmings; we are not—in the midst of motion—quietists. Rather, in the mightiness of the world we too want to be mighty . . . we are—in relativity—a part of God, we are divine, and create divinely all things. Our insignificance in universal motion is our grandeur of the One Motion which recognizes nothing as disparate, and no real parting of things. We belong to it so that in all the immeasurable world nothing can happen without us—nor, without us, is it completely One. *We are the One* in eternity and time.

T'ai-chi thus is simply the motion, the means of achieving the Oneness of life. It is the actualization of Maeterlinck's beautiful line, "We live in the sublime."

CHOU CH'I-CH'UN

Chou, the leading historian of Chinese boxing, had been edu-cated in the United States, and was an officer in the Chinese Air Force when I knew him. He befriended me from the start, intro-duced me to many boxers, and kept me aligned to the meaningful. Earlier I had purchased several books purporting to give the true history of Chinese boxing, and Sidney Tai had translated them for me. Representing a considerable investment in money and time, I took the results to Chou to peruse. He returned the documents to me telling me that they were worthless and that I should burn them.

Chou felt that in the old days boxing was a real art. The boxers trained hard and concentrated on their training. They were capable of creating great energy. Chang Hsiu-lin, a T'ai-chi and Pa-kua master who had died thirty years before, he regarded as superior to both Yang Shao-hou and Yang Ch'eng-fu. Chang would practice with a forty-pound weight attached to his index finger. Chou also felt differently about ch'i. He believed it was simply air, not energy. Skill and technique, not ch'i, were the important things. If one relaxed, sank, and reserved energy until the actual moment of strik-ing, it would be effective.

This slender little man told me that in Hopei Province Hsing-i was practiced in a hard, soft, and very soft manner depending on the locale, but in Shansi Province there was only one Hsing-i style,

which merged the hard and soft. Similarly—and this surprised me—
T'ai-chi was practiced at normal speed rather than in slow motion
in some areas of the mainland. (I saw Kuo Lien-ying's students
perform T'ai-chi at Taiwan University the day before I returned to
the United States, and their movements were at normal speed and
often quite fast. However, I never had the chance to ask Kuo
where his method originated.)[1]

It was Chou who told me of the so-called Wu style of T'ai-chi.
As taught in Southeast Asia, the postures and the arrangement vary
somewhat from the Yang method, but not overmuch, for Wu
Chien-ch'uan, its progenitor, learned in the Yang tradition and
changed the teaching but slightly. But what is called the Wu method
on the mainland is traced back to Wu Yu-hsiang (1812–80) and
descended through Li I-yu to Hao Wei-chen and Hao Yueh-ju
(thereafter called the Hao school) and to Sun Lu-t'ang (thereafter
called the Sun school). Wu Yu-hsiang purportedly synthesized the
old and new schools of Ch'en Chia K'ou and the big and small of
the Yang school. Originally, it had energetic jumping and slapping
of kicking toes, but these postures were deleted by Hao Yueh-ju to
enable older people to practice it.

Chou told me when he tossed the spurious documents back to
me that he would provide me solid historical data. He had been
writing for the Taiwan and Hong Kong media for years, and this
material he made available to me. In my other books I have made
extensive use of his material, and his significant article on the origin
of T'ai-chi appears here as appendix A.

KAO FANG-HSIEN

There was a derisive statement circulating among Westerners
during that period: "When the Nationalists came to Taiwan they
had more generals than privates and more privates than guns." The
implication, of course, was that the Nationalist army lacked fighting

ability. General Joseph W. Stilwell never believed this of the individual Chinese soldier. Nor do I. As a matter of fact, the Nationalists had some exceptional generals. Kao Fang-hsien was one.

Perhaps the best Shao-lin master in Taiwan, Kao lived in Taichung. Although on the wrong side of fifty, Kao was a living advertisement for his method. Big, strong, and tough, he gave me many
hours on several trips. His skill was so great that no one quarreled
with him. Kao was also reputed to be an excellent wrestler, but I
was never privileged to see his shuai chiao. He was a no-nonsense
sort but still laughed a lot.

Many of the southern forms of Shao-lin are forceful and brutish.
The northern, "orthodox" methods shown me by Kao were swift
and authoritative. He was aware of Japanese karate but put it down
smilingly. "My son will try to kick me," he once announced. His
tall son complied frantically and, let it be added, expertly. Kao

64–67. Kao Fang-hsien deflecting and attacking with combined fist and foot

parried the kicks easily, touching his son at each counter. "Kicking," he said, "should be a lesser part of fighting. If it is put first,
the fighter is vulnerable to counters."

Each time I worked with him I was astonished at how econom-
ical his techniques were (figures 64–67). For everything I tried, he
would show three or four ripostes, and yet each was a model of
simplicity. True sophistication, he said, was based on economy and
simplicity. What he did not say was that these qualities come only
from years of work under great masters. Again, I regretted my all
too few hours with this master Shao-lin boxer.

LIAO WAN-PAO

I learned White Crane boxing from Liao Wan-pao, a forty-year-
old native of Hsilo, the famed boxing center down island. Lithe,
slender, long muscled, Liao was brought to me by Liao Wu-ch'ang.
His skill was first-rate. From him I learned the Three Steps form,
which uses a half step, hands, elbows, and shoulders to make its
point (figures 68–71). The lead foot is never far ahead of the rear
foot; the attitude is lead heel aligned to rear toes. Both toes are
pinched in and movement is by sliding forward and back. The
turning in the art is truly effective, and the action of the feet is enhanced by the flailing of the arms: Five hand forms are used:

68–71. Liao Wan-pao in a basic White Crane movement

Ground hand — palm down
Water hand — palm up
Gold hand — knuckles vertical
Fire hand — backs up
Wood hand — palm down, fingers extended

Liao worked me hard for six months. The form looks strong, but he insisted that no force was to be used. The ch'i is gathered and released as necessary. It is paramount in this form that the feet and the arms be no wider than the shoulders and that the feet and arms move together. Later I was able to see other White Crane masters and to compare notes. Hung I-hsiang once suggested to me that this method was very vulnerable to kicks. I would amend this to say that because it is a relatively high closed-stance system it is defective against kicks targeted lower than the waist. Against high kicks of whatever kind it provides excellent position for blocking and countering.

CH'EN CHIN-SHENG

Through my association with Liao Wu-ch'ang and Hung I-hsiang I met and practiced several times with Ch'en Chin-sheng ("Young" Ch'en), middleweight champion of Taiwan for the three years 1958–60. Son of a Shao-lin boxer, Ch'en was all fight (figure

72. Ch'en Chin-sheng (with author) fooling around with a high kick he would never use in a fight

72). Although his technique was neither subtle nor very satisfying to me, it got results. William Ch'en, who won the lightweight championship in 1958, told me of seeing "Young" Ch'en resting before his final match that year; his face was almost entirely black-ened by the beating he had taken up to that point.

. I saw a couple of these tournaments. Some of it was almost ludi-crous. Many of the boxers "threw baseballs" (wild hooks) and made serious miscues by Western boxing standards. I showed a karateka from Okinawa films of a previous match between Hong Kong and Taiwan. He, too, was unimpressed, but then made the mistake of saying none of the boxers could have stood before the grace and force of his master. I remonstrated quietly that if karate had contact it would look little different; contact brings a new dimension that impinges on beauty. Any of the top twelve Chinese fighters in the film, I told him, could could do forms (*kata*) that would have left his master breathless, but in a real fight with the unrehearsed milling and pain (aye friend, there is the word) *kata* stands for little.

"Young" Ch'en worked in a drugstore on the second story of a building, and at noon each day would leave for lunch in an eccentric way: he would stroll out the window, land on the sidewalk, and walk away. Even the Chinese, who at times can be blase, must have received a start. I asked Ch'en about this and he disdained the technique. In Peking, he told me, there lived a famous boxer who dropped down from three stories onto an interior courtyard without making a sound when he landed. And Ch'en was no stranger to street fights; he had once bested eight men in downtown Taipei in a combined sword-fist-foot go (sword fights still occur in Taipei, death often deciding the issue).

When I hosted the high-ranking Korean karate master Shon Duk-sung and was showing some martial movies to him and some Chinese boxers, at a change of reel Ch'en stood up and challenged Shon. Another time, when Ch'en, Hung I-hsiang, and I were practicing together, Ch'en suggested in a friendly manner that I try conclusions with him. This would be an all-out go: hands, feet, boxing gloves. I countered that I would be happy to oblige using Western boxing rules or, alternatively, we could settle the issue with judo (he also practiced judo). He would not agree to this and so put the same question to Hung. Grizzled Hung laughed and agreed provided that Ch'en take off the boxing gloves. This was unsatisfactory to Ch'en and so nothing came of it. I regretted this denouement for it would have been an interesting, if sanguinary, battle. "Am I no a bonny fighter," wrote Robert Louis Stevenson, and the same can be said of Ch'en, a boxer tried and tested.

KAO SEN-HUANG

Kao Sen-huang, a friend of Liao Wu-ch'ang, was a fine boxer in the southern Shao-lin tradition (figure 73). I practiced many times with him. His fist work and low kicks were excellent. He was a mainstay on the Taiwan team that had met the combined Hong Kong-Macao team in the mid-fifties; he won with a kick that broke his opponent's leg. Kao could squash a potato with one hand and his brick breaking technique was crisp and effective.

73. *Kao Sen-huang: simple, direct, powerful*

Several times he traveled with me to meet various boxers around the island. He once told me that his family had hired the leading boxer in southern Taiwan, Wu Ta⁄ch'ao, to teach him Shao⁄lin when he was younger. Wu came but spent the first six months in the kitchen sampling the cook's wares. The family waited him out, however, and Kao finally got the instruction he craved.

Wu I saw only once. He sat in the midst of a crowd listening to a medicine hawker, one of his students. Liao Wu⁄ch'ang disliked Wu and told me that he had once been a great boxer but had fallen on poor days and had been reduced to selling medicine. Old age, injuries, and illness had crippled him. Still he taught, reminding me of Michel Fokine's ballet teacher, Christian Petrovich Johansson, in his eighties: "Tall, hunched with age, hardly able to move, he taught us how to dance." Fokine and his colleagues had to help their mentor up the stairs. And even sitting before them, he could scarcely speak, and had to do most of the teaching with his hands. It took the greatest concentration to hear and understand his instruc⁄tions. Significantly, Fokine felt it was worth it. And so did Wu's students. He died in 1963.

10. Teachers in Southern Taiwan

Becoming is more important than the being.
PAUL KLEE

In March, 1961, Liao Wu⁄ch'ang, Peter Ch'en, and I traveled to southern Taiwan for a week to visit leading boxers. Many times I journeyed outside Taipei to partake of a single teacher's offering, but this trip brought me into contact with many teachers in a short period and broadened my perspective perceptibly. The trip was scheduled so that I could see the endless variety and value of Chinese boxing. Thus it was largely for me. But by their deep interest, my Taiwanese colleagues revealed that they too derived much from what they saw. We did not see all we wanted to see. We put off seeing the Shao⁄lin master of the Bamboo Mountains until another time, a time that never came. At Hsilo we got little but worked up a debt that we were able to collect later.

LIN KUO⁄CHUNG

We first visited Lin Kuo⁄chung, a seventy⁄seven⁄year⁄old White Crane master, in Hoube (figure 74). A farmer, Lin was born in Fu⁄chou, Fukien Province, and had come to Taiwan fifty years before, bringing with him the two⁄hundred⁄year⁄old White Crane method of Fang Shih⁄p'ei. I performed a basic Shao⁄lin form, and Lin's son responded with a primary White Crane form similar to that of Liao Wan⁄pao in Taipei.

Master Lin explained the sequence of mastery in his method.

74. White Crane master Lin Kuo-chung

First the novice is taught the basics. He then practices these by him-self for three or more years. Following this, if he has made sufficient progress, he engages in free fighting in which actual contact is made. Few injuries result, however, since the skill of the boxers is on a common level and self-neutralizing. Special medicines are used to sustain the boxers, and these are taken internally as well as applied externally.

To my question about the value of ch'i in his system, Lin re-sponded that it was most important. There were, he said, four kinds of ch'i used by him.

> The ch'i of inhalation ("swallow")
> The ch'i of exhalation ("spit")
> Holding ch'i up ("to float")
> Holding ch'i down ("to sink")

The ch'i principle is applicable in the use of leg techniques as well as in the use of hands. However, I saw no leg techniques in the system, only hands. In fact, I felt at that time that the White Crane boxers were so hand oriented that they might be disadvantaged by an oppo-site number utilizing the legs. Hung I-hsiang later stated the same view to me.

The mind is paramount. The fingers are geared to the breath, and the eyes look steadily ahead. Lin held that the ch'i is not stored in the navel but comes from the sole of the foot through the navel to the head, where it is used as the occasion demands.

TUNG CHIN-TSAN

Before going to Chiai to see Tung Chin-tsan, we stopped at Peikang. The temple there is over four hundred years old. Kao Sen-huang met us, his hands beat up as usual from his nefarious medicine selling. He leaned toward short boxing, using fingers for closer and fists for longer work. For extremely close quarters he advocated the elbow. He reminded me that in the three-finger poke, boxers used to throw a small dagger hidden behind the middle finger. The leading master in Peikang was not present, but his stu- dents performed Lion and Ball, Conquer Tiger, Yellow Dragon, and Cherry Blossom boxing for us. Only the last was noteworthy. It began like a fast White Crane form, and the fist work was excep- tionally quick. The old master in this form, Liao said, could slide thirty feet in his leg attacks.

The next day we journeyed to Chiai to see Tung, alias the Golden Dragon. This one has a reputation throughout the island, and his students, I was told, numbered over ten thousand. Some were mem- bers of the underworld Black Dragon Society, and Tung himself had recently spent three years in a corrective labor camp as a result of being implicated with them. A slender bright-eyed man, Tung welcomed us warmly. He told me that he was versed in the boxing of the Wutang and Shao-lin Mei-hua (Plum Blossom) schools, and his teachers had been the monk Wei-chen, Ch'en Yu-an, and the monk Ho Feng of Fukien; Hsiao-Yao-t'ing of Kiangsi; the monk Pai-ho Shou-feng-mu of Yunnan; Lu Ta-ting of Tai- wan; and some Japanese masters. He had visited, he said, the Shao-lin Temple in Fukien and he considered the acme of boxing to be the soft, counteracting art.

The demonstration Tung and his students gave was a resounding disappointment. In *judogi* they presented a clumsy and silly version of *goshin-jutsu*. Their demonstration of several boxing forms was

75-76. The "Golden Dragon," Tung Chin-tsan, working with a wooden dummy

better, but something you write home about only to your mother-in-law. Subsequently, we visited his farm and watched him work on a huge sandman and a wood dummy (figures 75-76). Here the Gold Dragon really shone, so much so that later I had Liao build me a wood dummy at my house at Grass Mountain. His attacks were swift, crisp, and sure and served to mitigate the doubts cast on his boxing ability by the pseudo judo.

CHANG SHIH-JUNG

From Chiai we went to Tainan. The chief instructor at the large Chinese air force installation there, Chang Shih-jung, was a master of the three nei-chia. Fiftyish, rather handsome, and most congenial, Chang was a mainlander taught by Cheng Huai-hsien of Hopei. He was forthright in discussion and demonstration and provided us with an informative Sunday afternoon. He and his fifteen-year-old son showed T'ai-chi, Hsing-i, and sword work (figure 77). The T'ai-chi was of the Yang school and differed little from that of most orthodox teachers. The Hsing-i, however, was a model of celerity.

77. *Chang Shih-jung, master of internal boxing*

After doing the five basic forms, Chang showed the snake style, lowly crouched, in which the arms are used perpendicularly; the dragon style, which resembles *pi-ch'uan* in a deep crouch and in which the action is down to up; the chicken style featuring the elbow; the camel style, in which when attacked with a two-hand hook, you block and use two fists to the midsection; and the hawk, horse, tiger, and bear. Chang's basic five incorporated more power than Yuan Tao's (which is not to say that they were more effective), and his fingers were often perfectly perpendicular. He told us that both ways of holding the fingers are correct, because they are for different uses. He insisted that the fist should be lined up with the nose and that pressing must be combined with a punch downward so that there is a reaction upward from the opponent's feet (Wang Shu-chin, Yuan Tao, and Kuo Fang-chih all stressed this to break the opponent's root). While other comments also tended toward the familiar—Pa-kua enables you to make an opponent dizzy as a prelude to your attack; the long boxing of form practice becomes short boxing in a real fight—the insight of the new and the solid reinforcement of the old made for a pleasant afternoon.

Chang headed the workshop of the Taiwan Municipal Chinese Boxing Committee; he gave me its catalogue. The curricula covered T'ai-chi, Hsing-i, and Pa-kua. Each had four levels: primary, middle, advanced, and research; and the students were graded. The first three levels took three months each but the last had no time limit. Each step embraced twenty-four hours in the three months. The instruction was broken down as follows:

	Primary	*Middle*	*Advanced*	*Research*
T'ai-chi	basic steps	fixed step, pushing hands	moving step, pushing hands	boxing and weapons use
Hsing-i	five basic styles	twelve styles	close fighting	continuation
Pa-kua	fixed steps	moving steps	changing steps	continuation

WU KU-TS'AI

In Tainan the following day we met Wu Ku-ts'ai, a fifty-five-year-old Taiwanese, who had been a student of the Shao-lin school of Yung Ch'un County, Fukien, since he was fourteen (figure 78). A no-nonsense, not especially amiable type, Wu did not hold with the *nei-chia* of north China. Although he did not appear physical, his system certainly was. His Shao-lin was extremely short, making much use of two parts of the wrist to attack vital points. It used the feet, but the knees were always well bent and the attacks kept low. He used a wooden post with but one protuberance on which the fists, wrists, and forearms were hardened (figures 79–80). A student

78. *Wu Ku-ts'ai*   79–80. *A student using Wu's post*

demonstrated Three Tigers, a short boxing emphasizing the elbows and the short body hook of Western boxing. Another lad presented Sound Many Defenses, a longer boxing, lower, and stressing the sword hand (chop). In Wu's system elbow and shoulder work appeared first-rate and were buttressed by fine turning movements. His regimen was rigorous. Only family members were taught, starting at the age of sixteen. The training took three hours a day and involved using iron balls for finger power, plus contact. Wu said that previous hardening and the medicine he used internally and externally prevented injury. He ended by saying that he believed in the ch'i but that it would only come through long and hard physical—as opposed to light ch'i-kung—practice.

LI KIM-SUI

Li Kim-sui, short, smiling, and wiry, owned a restaurant (complete with girls, some of the prettiest I saw in Asia) and considerable farmland around Tainan. The fourth-generation master of Eighteen Buddha Boxing, a method purportedly brought to Taiwan by a monk-expert who had escaped from the Fukien Shao-lin Temple more than one hundred years ago, Li's teacher was Chao Ch'ing-shih from the P'eng-hu Islands. The 18 can be separated into three parts of three steps each: forward and then turning and retracing the steps equals 18. The 18 are linked up into various combinations to make a total of 108 forms.

Li at forty-four was short and had the warrior look (figures 81–84). He was distinct from most other boxers on at least two counts: (1) he did not smoke, and (2) his method gave priority to offensive tactics. His shoulders were like iron from his workouts on a fixed sandbag. His hands, too, bore the marks of training three hours daily throughout many years. He told us that formerly he trained his hands by using iron balls atop a fire but now only heats the balls. Self-deprecating (unlike most boxers) Li was a joyful giver.

81-84. *A sampling of the Shao-lin of Li Kim-sui*

Hung I-hsiang, in his glorious fashion, responded with "there are no good boxers in Tainan" when I told him later I had met a splendid master there—then thundered, "What was his name?" When I identified Li, Hung strangely subsided, saying, "Oh, he is my good friend." But then he wondered aloud why Li had talked to me; presumably Li's teaching was fairly secret and he permitted himself few students. The answer to this first meeting reposed with Liao and his leverage. My subsequent talks with Li I like to think resulted from a rapport which I felt and he seemed to share.

Li strongly believed in ch'i (why else put your hands into red-hot iron balls?). The essence of his method is that ch'i cannot go to the eyes or genitalia (some old texts also exclude the cheeks); thus, these are the best targets. From a moderately deep stance going often into a cat stance, he advanced rapidly, clawing at the eyes with his right hand while his left hand either protected his middle or clawed at the groin. Hands could be alternated, and a fist to the opponent's midsection varied the attack. To further jumble the opponent's defense, the speed of the attack varied between fast and very fast. Truly, his was a system exemplifying the fact that a good offense is the best defense. There were simply too many arcing hands and powerful fists put up too quickly for the antagonist to cope. To see the wild and whirling swirl of arms was thrilling, and also somewhat frightening.

CH'EN SHU AND CH'EN YING-CHAO

In Kaohsiung we met Ch'en Shu, who was forty-two years old, and had trained since he was twelve (figure 85). He was thin, wiry, and fast with his feet. Disdaining the *makiwara*, he advocated free fighting at full throttle with no protective gear. When Liao railed at him for having Wu Ta-ch'ao's picture on the wall, Ch'en appeared somewhat abashed about it. But he did not take the picture down.

We then visited Ch'en Ying-chao, a Chinese doctor (figure 86). He looked like a typical small-town dentist in the American Mid-west. Just a year on the right side of sixty, Ch'en had a peculiar but effective art that consisted of flailing with his hands off his chest onto the forehead and groin of the antagonist. The assaulting mem-ber was the flat top-fist of each hand, singular in itself since Cheng Man-ch'ing once told me that this area of the hand was very vul-nerable. But through dint of thousands of hours against a fixed sandbag on the wall, Chen had so hardened these parts that, when young, he could break a one-inch-thick stool with either of them. A stool, about $1\frac{1}{2}$ inches thick, of quite hard wood in the room bore his imprint half way through, permitting me to put my fist into it. Ch'en also used his feet, but only the inner surface in a low kick-ing probably designed to keep the opponent centered so that the top-fist could do its nefarious work. Since the head was perhaps his

85. Ch'en Shu

86. Ch'en Ying-chao: top-fist specialist

prime target, I asked Ch'en about its use as a weapon. He responded that only in close quarters is the use of the head warranted; otherwise it is very dangerous for the user. He also thought it perilous to tele⁄graph with your shoulders; they should be kept immobile until the moment of the attack. Know your enemy and react quickly with a few well⁄mastered skills: this was the essence of his teaching.

HSILO

After Kaohsiung we moved on to Hsilo, where there is a rich heritage of boxing. This area once contained the most affluent men in Taiwan, men who employed the best boxers as their teachers. This tradition dated back three centuries. About 180 years ago the heavy concentration of boxers here split into three groups headed by the most expert boxers. These were: the Resurrection Society, Liao Wu⁄fang's Southern Shao⁄lin Center, and the Assiduous Learn⁄ing Hall.

Only forty years ago the area still had many boxers capable of cutting through stone with bare hands or making a hole in one⁄inch⁄thick wood with a finger. Li Chi, an old boxer who died in 1960, had lived there. It was said that he could put his arm into the ground up to his elbow and could even catch a fly with his chop⁄sticks. At the time of my trip, however, training was lackadaisical. Most boxers had taken jobs, and whatever systematic instruction existed was being given on a personal basis.

We had an interesting time here. After finally cornering five masters, we spoke for four hours with them. (Ch'en said that Kao talked too long; we had our chance early on but his garrulousness ruined it). I doubt this. The exchange was all in Taiwanese, of which I was almost totally ignorant, but I sensed an antipathy to me. Finally, only one of the masters, Liao Hsin⁄hai, agreed to perform. This seventy⁄two⁄year old did a Shao⁄lin form misnamed Inner Pa⁄kua, which was singularly unimpressive; it merely looked like a terribly old man doing his morning exercises. I came away dis/heartened.

It hit Liao Wu/ch'ang harder. He lost a little face. He told me later that Thomas Liao, the leader of the Taiwanese independence group, then in Japan, was a native of Hsilo. In fact, during the 1947 revolt against the Nationalist government the cream of the Hsilo boxers had been exterminated. The United States government had sided with Chiang Kai/shek, I was a part of that government, there/fore they owed me nothing, not even hospitality.

They owed me nothing, but they did owe something to Liao Wu/ch'ang (Hsilo is full of Liaos so he probably had many rela/tives there); at least they owed him for their discourtesy. And they may have felt something for me, too, for two months later I was told that they were sending a group of boxers to Taipei to put on a show for us. There in the courtyard of a temple into which at least two thousand people were jammed, the Hsilo boxers performed for four hours in a driving rain. And it was worth waiting for; it was splendid. That night I saw some of the best Shao/lin I had ever seen. One husky boxer in particular stood out; he did his forms while thrusting a wooden beam into his abdomen. At one point I was invited to speak. I saw the uselessness: there was no public address system; there was rain, noise, and multitudes (most of whom were not listening); and there was Peter Ch'en as an interpreter (I always suspected he understood every third word in English). The upshot was that I was tempted to do what Cary Grant did when surrounded by a myriad of thugs in *Gunga Din*: he shouted, "All right, you're under arrest." But I resisted the temptation and merely said, as I now reiterate, a fond thank you to the Hsilo boxers.

CHANG I/TE

Chang I/te of Taichung maintained that he rather than Lin Kuo/chung of Hoube was the true Taiwan inheritor of the Fukien White

87–89. White Crane master Chang I-te showing two postures and deflecting author's attack

Crane method (figures 87–89). An intelligent and impressive man, Chang operated a jewelry store and was expert at jewelry design. He stated that Lin deferred to him by sending him students. Chang delineated the origin and history of White Crane Boxing as follows.[1]

Fang Ch'i-niang, the daughter of Fang Shih-yu of Fukien, a teacher of a soft method of Shao-lin, was expert in that method and in stick fighting two hundred years ago. One morning while she was combing her hair, a white crane came to rest just outside her window. She playfully poked at him with her stick, but he used his wings to divert the attack, causing her to drop the stick. Angered, she picked up another stick and with all her skill launched another attack. This time the crane broke her stick into two pieces. Astounded, she implored the white crane spirit to come and guide her boxing. At this the crane made a noise (imitated to this day by White Crane boxers). Next day the crane in the guise of an old man came to teach her. Under his tutelage she mastered the method after a long period.

Her servant, Chen Li-shu, learned the method from her for several years, after which he returned to his hometown to teach the villagers so that a threat by bandits could be quashed. Ch'en taught his first class of twenty-eight students, and they later came to be called the "Twenty-eight Heroes" for their success in ridding the place of bandits. One of the twenty-eight, surnamed Li, escaped to Taiwan during the Manchu troubles, came to Tansui, but died without teaching. The White Crane movement became a full-fledged secret society replete with recognition signals. For example, its boxers used two fingers of the rising right hand for this purpose. To advance three steps symbolized the intention to overthrow the Manchus; to retreat three steps connoted revenge.

Each of the twenty-eight got copies of a secret work. A student, surnamed P'eng, of one of the twenty-eight inherited a copy. Once P'eng, his student, and a monk retired to a temple for a thorough restudy of the book. After a while, a friend of his father, a Shao-lin expert, went to the temple to ask P'eng to return to the village to tend P'eng's ailing father. There the friend asked P'eng to demon-strate the method. P'eng complied. The Shao-lin expert thereupon berated P'eng for the softness of the art. He then showed his hard method. P'eng laughed at this: "Your method is so hard; how can you function in a real fight?" There being no alternative, they squared away. In the boxer's first rush, he could not penetrate P'eng's defense, and was pushed into a bed, breaking it. Two sub-sequent all-out efforts, likewise fruitless, further damaged the furni-ture. Whereupon the Shao-lin expert recognized P'eng's skill and bowed before him. This made P'eng famous throughout Fukien.

Chang's grandfather was expert in Dog Boxing (*kou ch'uan*), in which the opponent is pulled to the ground, scissored, and kicked. Chang told me that the only way to fight a Dog boxer is to stay clear of him and throw things at him; above all, never close with him. Despite his ability, Chang's grandfather was beaten by a White Crane boxer. This led the grandfather to take Chang's father to P'eng's grandson, a White Crane adept at the age of thirty. The grandson got into some kind of trouble, and Chang's father helped him to move to Foochow, learning from him for two years. For his kindness, P'eng presented the father a copy of the book, and he brought it with him to Taiwan nearly seventy years ago. Chang inherited the teaching from him. He had not used the method much in recent years, although it had pulled him through many scrapes in earlier years. About thirty years before he had been challenged to a friendly match by the judo instructor at Taichung Middle School, Chuang Szu (fifth-dan). During the fight, he would not let the judo master take hold and defeated him soundly.

Chang spelled out the principles of White Crane Boxing. It requires the uniting of sinew, spirit, ch'i, power, and strength. The art is based on the circle: everything should accord with roundness.

The biceps (tiger) should rise.
The forearms (dragon) are always rounded.
The rising thighs (leopard) are combined with the claw hand, which has power in two points.
The first two fingers (snake hand) provide the direction for the body to follow.

White Crane is essentially a soft boxing, but it incorporates the hard as well. In this connection, Chang told me that it was not necessary to wiggle the fingers, as many did, but that the spring power derived from the soft and pliable postures was a prerequisite for success.

The posture requires five points on a line:

Buttocks to heel of rear foot
Nose and knee
Elbow and toe of front foot
Toe of rear foot and heel of front foot
Shoulders and fingers

"OLD MAN" WANG

After leaving Taichung we went to Tachia, where we met the Shao-lin boxing "boss" of the area, a man surnamed Wang. I never learned his given names; the others always called him "Old Man" Wang (figure 90).

While sitting in his modest home, he told his story. From child-

90. "Old Man" Wang

hood he had studied boxing in the Chiai area. Once by means of his skill he had captured a thief who had stolen goods from a Japanese circus and whom the Japanese police could not apprehend. Thereupon, the circus offered Wang a job as guard. While traveling with the circus he met Huang Fei-hu, an outstanding boxer. Huang had come to Taiwan from Shantung and had taken a job selling milk, preferring not to teach boxing. Huang's penchant for heroin got him into trouble with the police. Wang was able to effect his release, and a grateful Huang taught him boxing. After only sixty-two days, however, Huang received a letter requiring his return to Shantung, but he had no money to make the trip. Wang, who had housed and fed Huang for two months, gave him the equivalent of one thousand American dollars. For this generosity Huang presented him with a secret manual at the ship.[2] This small volume, Wang said, had been the basis of his teaching ever since.

I asked the seventy-year-old Wang what special skills Huang had given him. He answered that he had learned much. Huang had had exceptional gripping power; in grasping one seeks the "one-thousand-pound power." For this he urged use of a six-foot length of bamboo, which is grasped and turned, one hand fighting the other. Huang also had a fine Hawk Hand derived from vase catching and holding with the fingers. According to him, Huang's greatest skill was to jump twenty feet high without bending the knees. Wang had been successful in this skill but never to the same degree.

In the section on "Light Work" in his book *Wu-shu Nei-wai-kung*, Wan Lai-sheng mentions this method. One first practiced the Swan: using only the flex of the body, one attempted to jump without bending the knees. With this restriction, a one-inch jump was the equivalent of one foot. By dint of daily practice (although the twelve repetitions reported by Wan seem inadequate), one gradually could soar over obstacles twenty feet high. Coupled with the vertical jump was the Swallow, in which the flex of the knees is added to that of the body, and the boxer becomes able to long-jump over twenty feet from a standing posture. Finally, weighted clothes and shoes are used, and after ten years the long jump can be extended to thirty feet, even with the added weight. Such feats are clearly beyond our ken, defying as they do the longest recorded Olympic jumps taken at full gallop. They certainly smack of exaggeration, but if reduced by half still represent skills unavailable currently.

Wang had had over one thousand students. Moral character, he said, was a requirement for tuition. None of his students had ever gotten into trouble. A traditional doctor, he had, after an earthquake thirty years ago, treated two thousand people with those huge gnarled hands, the hallmark of the Shao-lin boxer.

AND STILL OTHERS

I saw the Shantung boxer Wang Shung-t'ing only once. This was on an occasion when I filmed performances by more than twen-ty-five leading boxers on Taiwan. He was a swarthy man with evil eyes, but his demonstrations were truly peerless. He performed a drunken boxing form in which one pretends to be tipsy in order to lure an opponent close, then demolishes him. He also showed Mantis Boxing, a linear ripping form in which the elbows are given full play, and T'ai I Sword. Liao Wu-ch'ang told me that he was an underworld figure of note and that on the mainland he had killed men with the sword. I set in motion several approaches to persuade Wang to teach me, but none worked. I was rejected by other boxers but this rejection disappointed me the most.

Another who was not enraptured with my charm was P'an Wen-tou, a police instructor in ch'in-na. Rather obese, awkward, and quite dogmatic, P'an fought my ideas on standardization of boxing, on which I wrote an article for a Chinese magazine. My choosing Han Ch'ing⁄t'ang as a ch'in⁄na instructor may have been part of his problem (let me be didactic: if there is someone you dislike, *you* have a problem). Or perhaps it was because I criticized his methods, many of which were cornball American techniques out of a special forces manual. Another was Lei Hsiao⁄t'ien, a boxer and author of a book on the art; it was said of his grandfather that he could repulse clubs with chopsticks. And there was the medico, whose surname was Ma, who had successfully treated ten thousand Taipei folk and who performed a sword dance derived from a dream; we were polite and did not tell him that a man should dream better.

Another doctor who taught a Taoist health method was Liu Chu⁄chiang. His method had the formidable title "Introversive Centripetal Contraction Physiotherapy" and stressed a quiet static exercising to promote the venous flow to the heart (centripetal), as opposed to vigorous pursuits that caused blood to flow through the arteries to the limbs (centrifugal). Liu's method for stimulating endocrine secretions, so that the sexual organs are brought under control and such maladies as nervous prostration, impotency, and nocturnal emissions (not to mention foreshortening of the sexual act) are corrected, is quite simple. While standing (the technique can be done lying down and sitting as well), the legs are at the width of the shoulders and the knees are slightly bent. Place the hands (the thumb of the right held by the left and the four fingers of the right placed on the back of the left) lightly below the navel. Gaze at a point on the ground ten feet ahead. Hold the breath in the belly and stop breathing. Contract the anal sphincter. After ten seconds re⁄lease the contracted muscles, exhale lightly, and return to a normal standing position, the hands extended by the thighs and the eyes looking directly ahead. Inhale lightly, bend the knees, and repeat. Do this twelve times in the morning and evening.

This contraction is practiced in various forms of boxing. This would seem empirical evidence that it has hygienic benefits beyond the sexual. There can be no disputing the latter. One boxer I knew used it and saved a rocky marriage. His comment borders on poetry: "Why win all day and lose at night?" Another claimed the dubious honor of being charged double at a Peit'ou house of prostitution because he "took too long." A leader in the Nationalist govern- ment coupled both attributes: at sixty-eight years of age he looked forty, had a beautiful complexion, jet black hair, lithe and youthful movements, and a string of college girl modern-day concubines . . . And there was the detective Mu Nai-hsu, who could climb vertically up the exterior of a house like T. E. Lawrence never could.

My research was not limited to Taiwan. I visited Singapore and Hong Kong several times to seek out quality boxers and boxing material, always with mixed results. I once visited a T'ai-chi hall in Singapore run by a nephew of Wu Kong-yi. The system derives from the Yang style and the arrangement is quite similar. Watching, I found these differences: the postures were done more speedily, the players stood higher, their coccyges were not plumb erect, and their heads were awry. The nephew showed his *t'ui shou*, which proved forceful but used too much hand and wrestling maneuvers. I marked the system off as ineffective but to be sure asked to push hands with the nephew. This could not be done, of course, but he served me up a bulky senior student. I pushed him about easily.

I next repaired to a school run by Hung Sheng-hsien, a former White Crane boxer who had studied assiduously under Cheng Man-ch'ing in Taiwan. Huang was in Sarawak, so I missed seeing him. But his students were first-rate and the T'ai-chi, quite correct. Huang in 1970 bested a wrestler, and was given some publicity for this feat. In Taiwan he was regarded as a fine boxer, losing only once that I know of (to Wung Yu-ch'uan, an excellent wrestler and T'ai-chi adept).

In Hong Kong I sought out the family of Tung Yin-chieh, a student of Yang Ch'eng-fu. His daughter Jasmine Tung, the acme of courtesy, spoke with me at length. Her older brother, Tung Hu- lin, was in Singapore at the time. Their club was a clean, well-lighted and mirrored place, but Jasmine told me that she taught chiefly at private homes. Her father, she said, had learned from Yang Ch'eng-fu for twenty years (from the age of seventeen to thirty-seven). When he died he left three trunks of manuscripts, but her brother kept them under lock and key. She said that it was not Wu Kong-yi but his father, Wu Kam-chin, who had studied under Yang. It was a toss-up on who would win at pushing-hands, her father's students or Wu's students. All the while we talked, the practice went on. The postures were correct if not exceptional. There was much pushing but no uprooting. Her young cousin was leading the practice and fending off senior students. Three times I asked to try conclusions with him but, after agreeing, she rambled on. I thought she was waiting until the session was over so that no face would be lost. But when it ended and the students started to drift away, up she got and said as pert as you please, "Mr. Smith, it's been so nice having you. I hope you can come again." Though I was in and out of Hong Kong several times thereafter, I never did.

In Hong Kong I also spent two days with Ni Mo, a Shao-lin teacher. Small and stout, his system was straight southern Shao-lin with admixtures of White Crane and Mantis. Although he himself impressed me as a man able to acquit himself well in the street, his method was unexceptional. This is not to say that there was no great boxing in Hong Kong—only that in several trips using many inter-mediaries I was never able to find it. My biggest find there was to be told by a fine arts store owner that the original thirteen T'ai-chi postures, an heirloom finely crafted in wood, had been offered to him for sale by two brothers for several years. But each time he got a customer to meet their price, they rejected the offer. I asked him to set up a meeting for me with the brothers. He reported later that they had refused even to discuss it. I was left to wonder at the valuable thing (just as I regretted the fine Hong Kong boxers) that had es-caped me.

Afterword

Bertrand Russell, writing about hostility between individuals, has pointed out the following basic distinction:

> When it is said that the love of fighting is a part of human nature, there are two things which may be meant. On the one hand, anybody may be made angry by certain kinds of provocation: few men are so saintly as to display no annoyance if someone pulls their nose. On the other hand, there are in some people impulses of aggression and a positive pleasure in combat. It is only these people that constitute a problem, since the other people can be placated by the simple technique of not pulling their noses.

This sort leads us to learn to fight. Such motivation certainly stimulated my early endeavors in Western boxing, wrestling, and in judo, and it led me into Chinese boxing. But here I soon learned why both Quintilian and Seneca deprecated those who stultify the mind by overattention to the body. For this art, especially the internal, puts the mind first. The body is harshly subordinated. And thus the art becomes somewhat innocuous except as a form of self-training and discipline. In the end one's art becomes so inbred that one forgets it, except in the rare instance of having to use it.[1] And even then the response is carefully weighed so that the attacker is converted, not defeated.

A student came to a rabbi and said, "In the olden days there were men who saw the face of God. Why don't they anymore?"

The rabbi replied, "Because no one can stoop so low."

Jung ("One must stoop a little in order to fetch water from the stream of life") and Kazantzakis ("the gate of Heaven is very low") and Chinese boxing echo this truth. Such humbling cannot but bring life, love, truth, and peace.

The major world and individual problem facing us is aggressive violence. A military state is essentially a weak state, for the claim that its citizens have on it is peace, which cannot be gained by weapons. The solution is a rigorous pacifism. I have matured to the point now where I am a pacifist—alas, not one prepared to go the whole lamb yet, but one not apt to rush forward at the sound of the tired old shibboleths. There is almost no reason in the world to fight. But there is every reason in the world to know how to fight: it gives one Mark Twain's "confidence of a Christian with four aces." My thinking, which has evolved more from Taoist than from Christian teachings (I should have liked it to be otherwise), continues to mature. The boxing I espouse is part of that thinking, and I suggest that such a state is far more conducive to rapid assimilation of boxing than the ridiculously sanguinary approach most Westerners take to it. I hope this book in some small way affirms this truth. I remain one striving to become like the master Hsueh-chueh (ca. 713) wrote of:

> He meditates when walking and when sitting. Silent, speaking, moving, resting, his body is at peace. In the face of pointed swords he remains externally calm.

Appendix A: Chou Chi=Ch'un's Views on the Origin of T'ai=chi

There are four basic claims regarding the origin of T'ai-chi.

I. CHANG SAN-FENG AS CREATOR

This theory was strongly pushed by the school of Yang Lu-ch'an and is the most popular claim of the past fifty years. Subsequently, many writers uncritically accepted it. The claim briefly is as follows:

> Chang San-feng of the Sung dynasty was the first to teach T'ai-chi. Many years later Chang Sung-ch'i, native of Hai-yen, Chekiang Province, in the Chia-ching reign [1522–66] of the Ming dynasty was the most famous T'ai-chi boxer. Later, Wang Chung-yueh, native of the T'ai-hang mountains of Shansi Province, received the art. He taught Chiang Fa, and Chiang passed the method to Ch'en Ch'ang-hsing, native of Ch'en Chia Kou, Honan. Yang Lu-ch'an and his relative Li Po-k'uei of Kuang-p'ing went together to Ch'en to learn the art, and Yang finally became proficient in it. This is how Yang came to learn T'ai-chi. His school still has many supporters.

This claim actually was originated by Ming dynasty loyalist Huang Li-chou's *Nanlei Anthology*, in which the inscription on Wang Cheng-man's tomb is recorded as follows:[1]

> The boxing prowess of the Shao-lin school is widely known throughout the world. Since it is essentially an offensive system, however, it is possible to counter its methods. There has arisen a certain school, the so-called Inner School, which controls the enemy's action by calmness. When he attacks he is immediately unearthed by a counter. Thus, people call the Shao-lin method the Outer School and the latter method the Inner School. The founder of the Inner School was Chang San-feng of the Sung dynasty. Chang was a Taoist living on Mount Wutang in Hupeh Province. Emperor Hui Chung summoned him but he could not go because of

113

bandits. One night he dreamed of being taught a special kind of boxing by Emperor Hsuan Wu the Great. The next morning Chang killed over one hundred bandits by himself. A century later Chang's art prevailed in Shensi Province and Wang Chung was its most famous promoter. Ch'en Chou-t'ung, a native of Wen-chow, Chekiang, learned the art from Wang and then taught it in his hometown. During the Chia-ching reign of the Ming dynasty, Chang Sung-ch'i was the most famed advocate of this art.

We can find a similar record in the biography of Chang Sung-ch'i in the *Ningpo Chronicle* compiled by Ts'ao Ping-jen, a governor of Ningpo Fu in the Ch'ing dynasty. Nevertheless, neither on the tomb nor in the chronicle was it stated that Chang San-feng was the founder of T'ai-chi. We have Chang's biography, but in it there is no indication that he either founded or was skilled in T'ai-chi. Secondly, while we grant that Yang Lu-ch'an learned the art from Ch'en Ch'ang-hsing, the Ch'en family never spoke of Chang San-feng. Thirdly, the so-called Inner Boxing mentioned in Huang Li-chou's *Nanlei Anthology* bears no resemblance to the T'ai-chi of today.

From all these facts we must conclude that the claim that Chang San-feng founded T'ai-chi is not supportable. How then did this claim arise? It is known that Wang Chung-yueh, author of *Theory of T'ai-chi*, was a native of Shansi Province, and his name had just one more character than that of the Inner boxer, Wang Chung, a native of Shensi Province. This similarity in names and in provinces (they are pronounced almost the same) may have added to the confu-sion. Since Yang Lu-ch'an was not well educated, his promotion of the Chang San-feng thesis and his combining T'ai-chi with "Inner Boxing" was probably done in conjunction with some of his well-educated students such as Hsu Lung-hou and Ch'en Wei-ming, both of whom could have read the *Ningpo Chronicle* and the *Nanlei Anthology*.

II. THE FOUR SCHOOLS OF T'AI-CHI: HSU, YU, CH'ENG, AND YIN

This thesis was promoted by Sung Su-ming, already seventy years of age when the republic came into being. According to the book *Orthodox T'ai-chi Boxing* by Wang Hsin-wu, Sung Su-ming stayed at Yuan Hsiang-ch'eng's house as a guest for a long period. He was versed in the *Book of Changes* and skillful in T'ai-chi. He claimed that he was the seventeenth-generation lineal successor of

Sung Yuan-ch'iao. A man famed in boxing circles, Hsu Yu-sheng, estab-
lished the Peking Athletic Research Society mainly for the promotion of T'ai-
chi. Such capable boxers as Chi Te, Liu Ts'ai-ch'en, Lin En-shou, Chiang
Tien-ch'en, and Wu Chien-chuan taught there. When they heard of Sung
they went to try their skill, were all defeated, and bowed before him as students.
Sung told them that what he taught was from Sung Yuan-ch'iao's own work
Sung's T'ai-chi and Its Offshoots, in which the four schools are recorded in some
detail. According to Hsu Lung-hou's *Illustrated Explanation of T'ai-chi Boxing*,
the details were as follows:

A. Reverend Hsu Hsuan-p'ing, born in the T'ang dynasty [618–ca. 907]
in Chi-hsien, Anhwei, lived alone in a secluded place in Nanyang and
abstained from any cereal food or any other human diet. He was strongly
built with a beard dangling to his navel and hair reaching the ground. He
walked as fast as a running horse. He was often seen selling firewood in the
market and chanting.

In the same dynasty poet prodigy Li Pai looked for him but failed to find
him. At last Li wrote a poem at the Viewing Hill Bridge. The T'ai-chi
Hsu handed down was called *San-ch'i*, as it was composed of thirty-seven
movements. He taught his disciples one action at a time and when all were
learned linked them together into what came to be called *Long Boxing*. The
secrets were titled Eight-Word Song, Theory of Understanding, Powerful
Function of the Whole Body, Sixteen Essentials, and Song on Functions.
Hsu taught Sung Yuan-ch'iao.

B. Boxer Yu, a native of Ching Hsien, Anhwei Province, inherited his art
from Li Tao-tzu of the T'ang dynasty. His boxing was called Long Boxing or *Hsien T'ien Ch'uan*. Li later lived at Nanyen Temple on Mount
Wutang. He ate nothing every day but several pints of bran, and was called
Saint Li. Yu Ch'ing-hui, Yu I-ch'eng, Yu Lien-chou, and Yu Tai-yen
inherited the teaching of this school.

C. Ch'eng Ling-hsi founded Ch'eng's T'ai-chi school. A native of Hui-
chow in Anhwei Province, it was due to his efforts that Hui-chow remained relatively undisturbed through the period of Hou Ching's rebel-
lion. Emperor Yuan Ti of the Southern Liang dynasty [502–57] appointed
him governor of this district and titled him Chung Chuang (Loyal and
Brave) after his death. Ch'eng learned his art from Han Kung-yueh. Later

Ch'eng Pi got the secrets. Hsu Lung-hu remarks that Ch'eng later wrote a book titled *Loshui Anthology*, changed the name of this boxing to *Hsiao Chiu T'ien*, which comprised only fourteen movements, and also wrote *Yung Kung Wu Chih* (Five Principles on Training) and the song *Szu Hsin Kuei Yuan Ke* (Song on Return of the Four Instincts).

D. The T'ai-chi handed down by Yin Li-heng was called *Hou T'ien Fa*. He taught Hu Chin-tzu, native of Yang-chou, Kiangsu, and Sung Chung-su, a native of An-chou. It consisted of seventeen movements, most of them using the elbow. Although the movements bore different names, they were identical with those of previous T'ai-chi schools.

In the context of the Hsu, Yu, Ch'eng, and Yin schools, let us look again at Chang San-feng. Alias Chun Shih, Chang was a native of Liaoyang, a scholar of the Yuan dynasty [1286–1368] and a gifted calligrapher, painter, and poet. A magistrate of a district in Hopeh, he aspired for a secluded life and cared little for official promotion. He made a tour of Mount Paochi where the three peaks led him to rename himself San Feng-tzu. Chang's biographers, of whom there were more than ten, never said that he was a boxer. In the early Hung Wu reign [1368–98] of the Ming dynasty, he was summoned by the emperor but was delayed by bandits. In a dream Emperor Hsuan Wu the Great taught him a special boxing, which enabled him the next day to defeat the bandits. His boxing was then named the Wutang School or Inner Boxing. *Inner* actually means *Confucianly Scholastic* to differentiate it from the Outer style. This boxing consisted of Pa Men (Eight Directions) and Wu Pu (Five Steps). So it was also named *Shih San Shih* (Thirteen Operations). Chang Sung-ch'i and Chang Ts'ui-shan gained all the secrets from him. It was said that Sung Yuan-ch'iao, Yu Lien-chou, Yu T'ai-yueh, Chang Sung-ch'i, Chang Ts'ui-shan, Yin Li-heng, and Mo Ku-sheng went to seek Saint Li at Mount Wutang but they failed to find him. When they passed Yu Shui Palace they met Chang San-feng and all bowed before him. They studied under him for more than a month. Afterwards they kept in touch with him. According to this story the seven mentioned above were all disciples of Chang San-feng, but only the boxing taught by Chang Sung-ch'i and Chang Tsui-shan was called Thirteen Operations.

The claims of the aforementioned four schools have been disproved by Professor Hsu Chen, who said in his book *Distinguishing the False from the True in T'ai-chi Boxing*:

Hsu Hsuan-p'ing's life was recorded in the book *Beginning and End of Tales on Poems of the T'ang Dynasty* written by Chi Yu-kung of the Sung dynasty. But there is no hint there that Hsu taught T'ai-chi. Ch'eng Ling-shi's life can be seen in the historical *Ch'en's Book* and *South History*. There it was only mentioned that Ch'eng when young was famed for his prowess. He was able to travel more than sixty-five miles a day on foot and was skillful on a horse. Nothing was said, however, of his acquiring T'ai-chi from Han Kung-yueh. Ch'eng Pi was a high official candidate in the Sung dynasty and wrote a book titled the *Ming Shui Anthology*. Hsu Lung-hou's saying that he wrote a book called *Loshui Anthology* is wrong. No old records indicate that Ch'eng Pi was adept in fighting. The stories about Yu and Ying Li-heng are absurd. I have learned that the actions of Sung Shu-ming's T'ai-chi are similar to Yang's and the titles are nearly the same, the difference being that many repetitions of a given movement were eliminated. I also learned that Sung's method of pushing hands was nearly identical with Yang's. Also, some key points in *Sung's T'ai-chi and Its Offshoots* were copied from the writings of Wang Chung-yueh and Wu Yu-hsiang. Thus it is evident that Sung's T'ai-chi was learned from the Yangs. To claim another source is only deceit.

III. *CH'EN CHIA KOU*

A. *That Ch'en Pu Originated It*

Ch'en Hsin, one of a line of great Ch'en Chia Kou boxers in Honan Province, pushed this claim. In the preface to *Illustrated Explanation of Ch'en's T'ai-chi Ch'uan* is the following: "In the seventh year of the Hung Wu reign of the Ming dynasty founder Ch'en Pu in his spare time from farming and studying invented certain techniques based on the principles of T'ai-chi to teach his sons and grandsons how to acquire and maintain good health." This statement was later proved false by T'ang Hao. In his *Investigation of the Origin of T'ai-chi*, he said: "Ch'en's tombstone was set up by his descendants in the fiftieth year of the K'ang Hsi reign [1662–1722], Ch'ing dynasty. The inscription was written by his tenth lineal successor, Chen Keng, but there was not one word mentioned about Ch'en's invention of T'ai-chi." If valid, this significant fact would not have been neglected, especially since the Ch'en family was famed in boxing for several generations. Therefore, it appears that the claim for Ch'en Pu's being the founder of T'ai-chi was wrongly assumed by Ch'en Hsin.

B. *That Ch'en Wang-t'ing Started It*

This claim was begun by the historian T'ang Hao. Ch'en Wang-t'ing's offspring Ch'en Tzu-ming repeated it later in his *Ch'en's T'ai-chi*. In his *Investigation of the Origin of T'ai-chi*, T'ang Hao mentioned that Ch'eng Huai-san of Ch'en Chia Kou had a book on the genealogy of the Ch'en family. Beside the name of Ch'en Wang-t'ing, his ancestor of nine generations before, was this note:

> Ch'en Wang-t'ing, alias Tsou T'ing, officer at the end of the Ming dynasty and official candidate at the beginning of the Ch'ing dynasty. He was a famous boxer in Shantung, annihilated more than one thousand bandits, and was the founder of Ch'en's boxing and weapons arts. Born chivalrous, he left this verse: 'I box when unhappy, I work on the farm when needed.'

T'ang concluded that this proved that Ch'en Wang-t'ing created T'ai-chi. Moreover, T'ang continued, the same genealogy listed Ch'en Ch'ang-hsing, fourteenth generation, as a "boxing teacher" and his son, Ch'en Keng-yung, as "boxer." Both were popular T'ai-chi exponents. Further, the Ch'en family at Ch'en Chia Kou never learned external boxing from outsiders. T'ang cited these facts to support the claim of Ch'en Wang-t'ing.

This claim was also disproved by Professor Hsu Chen. In his book *Distinguishing the False From the True in T'ai-chi Boxing*, he stated that Ch'en's book mentioned boxing but did not specify T'ai-chi; therefore, what Ch'en Wang-t'ing taught was not T'ai-chi. The two notes that referred to Ch'en Ch'ang-hsing and his son did not refer to T'ai-chi but only stated that both were adept in boxing. Moreover, what the father and son learned was not necessarily what Ch'en Wang-t'ing taught originally. The Ch'en family's refusal to learn boxing from outside Ch'en Chia Kou does not mean that none of their ancestors had learned boxing from outside. I have an old manuscript of Ch'en's combat arts that has several chapters on weapon use, in which one note mentioned an origin in the Yu family. Also, on the club and spear arts, the operations were said to have originated from Wang Pei-ts'un of Hopeh. These data indicate that many of Ch'en's students learned outside combat techniques.

IV. *THAT THE FOUNDER IS UNKNOWN*

This thesis originated with amateur boxer Li I-yu in his *Brief Preface to T'ai-chi Boxing*, written in 1881. Since the third year of the Hsien Feng reign [1851–61] in the Ch'ing dynasty, Li had studied T'ai-chi from Wu Yu-hsiang. Wu first learned T'ai-chi from Yang Lu-ch'an and later from Ch'en Ch'ing-p'ing of Honan. The latter was the disciple of Ch'en Yu-pen, a famous boxer of Ch'en Chia Kou. Even at that time the founder of T'ai-chi remained unknown. Without evidence, the claim for Chang San-feng is entirely groundless. Nor is there better reason to credit the claim of Hsu, Yu, Ch'eng, Yin, or Chen Pu and Ch'en Wang-t'ing of Ch'en Chia Kou as the founder. What Li says is most acceptable.

According to Professor Hsu Chen's books (*Investigation of the True History of T'ai-chi Boxing* and *Distinguishing the False from the True in T'ai-chi Boxing*) and articles, the only reliable history for T'ai-chi is as follows.

The founder of T'ai-chi is unknown. Wang Chung-yueh, a native of Shansi Province was skilled in this style of boxing. Once as he was passing through Ch'en Chia Kou at Wen-hsien in Honan, he saw the villagers practicing boxing. After returning to his inn he made some offhand remarks on their skill. Almost all the villagers were surnamed Ch'en and were famous in the art of *pao ch'uan* for several generations. Some were displeased at the stranger's comments, and when he left the inn several challenged him to fight, and were soundly beaten. They were impressed and asked Wang to stop for a short period in the village and teach them his boxing art. Moved by their sincerity, Wang stayed a while with the Ch'ens and modified their long boxing into what he called T'ai-chi. Only the most intelligent of the Ch'en's were taught the more profound parts of this method. Finally Wang left but some of his art remained in Ch'en Chia Kou thereafter.

At a much later time T'ai-chi was divided into the new and old styles. A famous boxer named Ch'en Ch'ang-hsing was adept in the old style. When Ch'en performed he always kept his body upright like a wooden idol in a shrine, thus was called Peiwee (the name of a shrine piece) Ch'en. He handed down his art to his son Ch'en Keng-yun. At the same time another distinguished T'ai-chi boxer, Ch'en Yu-pen, created the new T'ai-chi style. He had many students, among whom his son, Ch'en Chung-sheng, and Ch'en Ch'ing-p'ing of Chao Pao Dzun were the most famous. One of the Ch'ens from Ch'en Chia Kou ran a drugstore at Yung Lien Hsien, Hopeh. The owner purchased two boys from Yung Lien as servants. One was Yang Lu-ch'an; the other, Li Po-k'uei. The owner of the store engaged Ch'en Ch'ang-hsing, a famed boxer, to teach his sons. Yang secretly watched the teacher at work and practiced with Li. One day Yang showed a new student how to perform, and the teacher, seeing, urged Yang to demonstrate all he knew. Ch'en sighed when Yang had finished, lamenting that the students he taught had learned little while this man he had not taught had learned much.

After that Ch'en taught Yang more enthusiastically than his own students. After several years Yang became expert. One day Ch'en recommended to his master that Yang be given fifty liangs of silver and freed. Yang left his teacher and returned to Yung Lien Hsien, where he worked in a drugstore and taught T'ai-chi for a living. Since he could defend and attack so capably, his boxing was termed *soft* or *slippery* boxing. The store owner, Wu Yu-hsiang, and his two older brothers were wealthy gentry of the district. Since they had an interest in boxing, they became close friends of Yang. After a while Wu learned the essentials of T'ai-chi. Not content with this, he went to Ch'en Chia Kou, where he wanted to learn something from Ch'en Ch'ang-hsing. On the way he stopped at the inn of Chao Pao Dzun to ask the landlord for Ch'en's address. When the landlord learned of Wu's intent, in order to have Wu stay longer so he could make more money, he praised Ch'en Ch'ing-p'ing highly. This pleased Wu. Immediately he visited Ch'en Ch'ing-p'ing from whom he learned that Ch'en Ch'ang-hsing's method was old style T'ai-chi, and Ch'en Ch'ing-p'ing's, the new style. Some of the explanations Wu got from Ch'en he had not heard from Yang.

So Wu remained there more than a month learning a great deal. Later, Wu's eldest brother, Wu Ch'iu-ying, became magistrate of Wuyang Hsien, Honan. His associates there, knowing of his interest in T'ai-chi, told him that there was a manuscript on T'ai-chi by Wang Chung-yueh at a certain salt store. Wu Ch'iu-ying read it, was pleased, and had one of his clerks copy it and send it to his youngest brother. After studying it, the younger Wu was inspired to write five articles, the titles of which were: "Thirteen Postures of Long Boxing," "Body Methods," "Four Secret Words on Combat," and so on. The second son of Yang Lu-ch'an, Yang Pan-hou, learned from Wu for a while. This gave impetus to the works of Wang Chung-yueh and Wu Yu-hsiang being spread through Yang's school. Wu also taught Li I-yu, his sister's son, and Li wrote five articles on the art, titled: "Brief Preface to T'ai-chi," "Secrets of Combat," "Importance of Practicing Combatives," and so on. He also taught the art to Hao Wei-chen.

By endorsement of Wu's older brother, Wu Ju-ch'ing, Yang Lu-ch'an went to Peking, capital of the Ch'ing dynasty, to teach T'ai-chi. In Peking, Yang was greatly admired for none could beat him. Later he was invited to teach in the Flags Battalion (Manchu Nobles' Athletic Camp). There his best disciples were Wan Ch'un, Ling Shan, and Chin Yu, one with powerful strength, one with great striking power, and one with skillful evasive tactics, respectively. Under Yang's order, all knelt down subsequently as students of his son Yang Pan-hou. Yang Lu-ch'an had three sons; the first died early, the second was Pan-hou, and the third, Chien-hou, the latter two of whom were great boxers.

Appendix B: Sun Lu=tang's Principles of T'ai=chi Ch'uan

1. Your head is held up so vitality can concentrate. The mind, not force, holds it up.

2. Your mouth is gently closed, your tongue touching the roof of the mouth.

3. Breathe regularly through the nose.

4. Relax your shoulders downward; if they go up, the ch'i goes up and will not sink.

5. Keep your elbows hanging down so the ch'i can sink. Bend them but feel as if you want to straighten them. If the elbows are not bent there is no energy and you cannot attack.

6. Your chest should be relaxed inward. If thrust out, the ch'i will not sink, you will be overbalanced, and your root will "float."

7. The waist is the master of the body: it must sink.

8. The weight is not shared equally by the two legs; one leg always holds most of the weight.

9. Breathe into the tan t'ien, but let it sink by itself, do not force it.

10. If you can practice with a quiet mind and a calm spirit your movement will be active and nimble.

11. Use *i* (mind) not *li* (force). Use your *i* and your *li* will follow. If you use only *li* the movement will be too slow.

Appendix C: Ch'i=Kung, Exercise of Internal Energy

Ch'i-kung, a method of health, is probably at least two thousand years old. The term translates "exercise (or work) of the internal energy." Both Buddhists and Taoists practiced its forms, as have boxers down the years. Here I want to describe some of the properties of the method, paraphrasing from Chiao Kuo-shei's *Ch'i-kung Yang-sheng-fa*.

The body is complex. Change occurs in seconds, the motivation for change resting in the ch'i. To normalize ch'i is to regulate the body. Ch'i-kung functions:

1. To keep yin and yang in equilibrium. Yin (stillness) changing to yang (activity) and back again characterizes both life and the body.
2. To harmonize blood circulation and air circulation.
3. To clear the passages, so that the blood flows unimpeded.
4. To cultivate the "real" air that keeps the internal machinery working. The "real" air must be preserved, conserved, developed, and reinforced. An experienced ch'i-kung exponent always feels rich with air and remains in high spirits.
5. To regulate the breathing. The frequency of breathing is reduced and becomes deep, slow, and regular.
6. To improve digestion. Ch'i kung by its action on the diaphragm massages the stomach and the intestines.
7. To improve blood circulation and the action of the heart. With regular practice, the number of white blood cells increases, the work of the heart decreases, and blood pressure drops.
8. To normalize the nervous system and to achieve control of the skin and muscles. This has been proved by tests.

Ch'i-kung has both static (*ching*) and moving (*tung*) postures. The latter may be seen in the *pa tuan chin* calisthenics or in T'ai-chi. The principles that follow are those governing the static but are equally applicable to the moving exercises.

In standing one may do so naturally or in the manner of holding a basketball.

123

In natural standing the knees are slightly bent and the legs are on a vertical line with the shoulders. Sink the hips a little, remain well rooted, and keep the upper body in perfect balance. Relax the back and waist and let the shoulders and arms hang downward. Then slightly bend the arms, let the palms face downward, keep the fingers apart, and curve them slightly. Close your eyes lightly and look to the lower front. The basketball stance is the same except that the arms simulate holding a ball. The distance between the hands is the width of the chest.

In sitting on a chair keep the feet on the ground and the upper body upright. Relax the back and the waist, curve the arms a little, and sink the shoulders slightly. Or one may sit normally with the legs crossed or with a single leg crossed in a half lotus posture. Lying may be done on the back or side.

Ch'i-kung requires that the mind be directed to a certain part of the body, an object, a matter, or a word. While concentrating, relaxation is required. The mind may be directed:

1. To a certain part of the body. There are three *tan t'ien*. The upper is located between the eyebrows; the middle is approximately 1.3 inches inward from the navel; and the lower, three inches below the navel, although some authorities locate it between the penis and anus. Beyond these there are other bodily points important in ch'i-kung. There is a point called *spot of life* between the second and third lumbar vertebrae, and one called *sea of air* about 1.5 inches below the navel, which some identify as the lower tan t'ien. The outside of each big toe is related to the liver and spleen in Chinese medicine and along with a point on the sole of each foot is used as an object of concentration.

2. To a certain object. Concentrate your mind on a flower, a leaf, or a picture, which should be more than fifteen feet away. As you concentrate, let your eyes close slightly.

3. To a certain matter. Concentration is enhanced if one fixes the mind on a poetic line, a lofty thought, or a religious idea.

Breathing is the heart of ch'i-kung. The breath is inhaled slowly, softly, harmoniously, and rhythmically through the nose and exhaled in the same way (the text appears to err in this, for in the exercises below only the mouth is used in exhaling). Naturalness and relaxation are necessary. While breathing you must direct your ch'i to the different points enumerated above through your *i* (intent). The breathing methods follow:

1. *Quiet Breathing.* The first way is the most natural. Simply calm oneself and breathe normally. The second way is deeper. The mouth is closed lightly, and as one inhales, the tongue goes up to the roof of the mouth. The breath is inhaled and led down to the middle tan t'ien by the i. After a short pause, lead it back up slowly and softly, dropping the tongue, and exhaling through a slightly open mouth. A third method is to count the breaths: "one" in inhaling a breath that is directed to the tan t'ien, kept there a moment, and "*hu*" on exhaling. The next breath is then "two" on inhalation and "*hu*" on exhalation. After thirty, a beginner should rest a while.

2. *Abdominal Breathing.* This is a more vigorous breathing causing the abdomen to expand and contract. The usual way is simply to breathe as above. In inhaling, the abdomen expands filling with air; in exhaling, it empties as the air is expelled through the mouth. There is another method which merely reverses the procedure: on inhalation the abdomen sinks slowly, expanding on exhalation. In both methods there is a distinct pause after each inhalation-exhalation, during which the mind is kept on the middle tan-t'ien. The parts may be stretched out progressively. The beginner may recite a word silently while inhaling, pausing, exhaling, and pausing; later, additional words are added, thus prolonging the process.

3. *Mind Breathing.* This method has three ways. In navel breathing one breathes as if the air comes in and goes out of the middle tan t'ien rather than the nose or mouth. In heel breathing one inhales the air, leads it to the middle tan t'ien, lower tan t'ien, along the two legs, and finally to the soles of the feet, reversing the process on exhalation. One can alternate by inhaling from the bottom of the feet, leading it up the legs through the lower tan t'ien to the middle tan t'ien, and reversing the process on exhalation. In body breathing one imagines that, in inhaling, the air swarms to the middle tan t'ien from all parts of the body and leaves the same way in exhaling. Alternatively, in inhaling one may imagine all the skin pores closing and in exhaling opening again.

An obsolete method is to recite various words audibly while performing various actions. This then is a sketch of ch'i-kung. Concentration and perseverance coupled with relaxation and naturalness are required in order to reach the acme of the art.

The methods may be strange to a Westerner. They are, however, eminently more sensible than some other ch'i-kung methods of which I have heard. In one form, the teacher uses a metal rod to hit the student's body to "open the junctions and joints so that air and blood can pass." In another, fire is breathed. And, in the most extreme, a method for general health published in a brochure by Ch'iao Ch'ang-hung, the student holds a stone weighing 1 pound fixed to his penis; gradually the weight is increased to 155 pounds.

Appendix D: T'ai=chi in the People's Republic of China

The Chinese communists have instituted several scientific studies of T'ai-chi. Before the rupture of relations with the Soviet Union in the early 1960s, several Russians were involved in the research. Professors I. Baichenko and G. I. Krasnoselsky of the Soviet Union found the art worthy of medical investigation. In 1957 a teacher was sent at Ho Chi-minh's invitation to North Vietnam. The communists have studied T'ai-chi particularly for medical use and have short-ened the number of postures from over one hundred to twenty-four and the time requirement from twenty minutes to five minutes.

China Sports (No. 2, 1963) reported that two doctors of the Shanghai No. 1 Medical College had conducted experiments for a year in an effort to evaluate T'ai-chi. Using 220 elderly people, they split them into two groups: one (Group A) practiced T'ai-chi regularly while the other (Group B) did not. The test results follow.

Test	Group A	Group B
Average pulling strength	86.2 kg.	63.4 kg.
Ability to touch ground without bending knees	87.2 percent	15.6 percent
Reaction time	0.205 seconds	0.268 seconds

The T'ai-chi group also excelled in average thigh measurement and the depth of subcutaneous tissue, but these tests are subject to methodological bias and in any event are not as significant as those cited above. Overall, the T'ai-chi group's performance closely approximated that of young adults.

But the government has not been entirely happy with T'ai-chi. This was made apparent in the Peking monthly *Hsin T'i-yu* (New Physical Culture) in April, 1965, which contained several articles calling for an eradication of feudal rem-nants still present in Chinese boxing, especially T'ai-chi. Workers in the new China, we are told, should study T'ai-chi not for self-defense but rather to improve physical fitness, to raise productivity, and to increase their ability to defend the fatherland. This puts the art squarely into the utilitarian context so necessary for the survival of any institution in the People's Republic of China today.

The articles indicate that all is not well in the martial arts that the party and government have promoted so assiduously since the takeover on the mainland. Workers leave their productive jobs to teach disciples in parks; impressionable youths are obsessed with worship of the obedience to a teacher; and the martial arts themselves are imbued with the "ideological poison of many feudal superstitions." In eradicating this poison, however, the state must strike down traditions nearly as old as China itself, beliefs and habits rooted in the triad of Buddhism, Confucianism, and, most importantly, Taoism. Still smarting from its defeat on the communes (in which, curiously, Chinese learned that Chinese were as individualistic as Frenchmen, exemplifying Chesterton's beautiful line: "The most sacred thing is to be able to close your own door"), in the Great Leap Forward, and in the Cultural Revolution, the state may not intend a direct confrontation soon on such practices, but the bodements are there to see.

What feudalistic remnants did the critics find remaining in T'ai-chi? The chief ones were as follows:

1. Superstitious belief in old men and dead men. This is blatantly anti-Confucian. Man is experience, and if you do not heed history, you repeat it. One author decries the fact that living masters are obeyed and dead masters are revered. He cites Ch'en Fa-k'o and Yang Shao-hou as examples of men who, living, had no following but, dead, command large schools. The author is wrong: both Ch'en and Yang were famous while alive. They had exceptional skill but neither chose to commercialize it. Worse than this specific, the author's main argument is awry. The best of the past masters urged their students to modify the art taught them, but only within a tactical context. The framework of principle must stand. The author seems to be urging an overthrow of principle in favor of a mechanistic physical exercise.

2. Vulgar practices and commercialization. Here the author narrates the gradations the student goes through in establishing and maintaining a relationship with a teacher who often obfuscates, stalls, and distorts the teaching, all the while making money. Alas, the author rings the bell on this aspect. In extenuation, let me say that the popular dissemination of T'ai-chi should permit a student suffering such nonsense to see the light and

to change teachers. Additionally, to go too far in upsetting this teacher-student relationship impinges on a Buddhist tradition, one which while it has its faults does have a habit of producing great boxers.

3. Spreading belief in feudal superstitions. Here the author tackles Taoism by attempting to dismember the philosophical rationale behind T'ai-chi. True, the art rests on esoteric foundations (the yin and yang, the ch'i, and so on). Some of the esoterica can now be explained physiologically; that which cannot may well give us hitherto unavailable insights into the mind and spirit of the human animal. The author castigates teachers who exaggerate the rewards of T'ai-chi. There are such teachers. But, at the same time, there are rewards. Given the pragmatic quality of the Chinese, at some point the teacher must stand and show, and at this time the student can weigh the advertisement against the performance. In ending, the author egregiously says: "The T'ai-chi teachers say, 'Wrong no man.' In actuality, this is imported reactionary thought that is divorced from class and class struggle." This is nonsense: the sentiment taught is one espoused by Buddhism and communism alike. Which leaves one with the sobering thought: what has happened to the author since he penned these lines?

Appendix E : Wu=Shu Forms in Taiwan

Over the centuries there have existed an immense number of kinds of Chinese boxing—at least four hundred. Some are extant; some have disappeared. Because of the wide interest in the masters and methods, I list below types that I was able not only to observe but also to record on 16-mm motion picture film. (A number of other films involving chiefly Taiwanese boxers remains uncatalogued.)

Boxer	Title
Students of Liao Wu-ch'ang	Lion Form
Liao Wu-ch'ang (Taiwan)	Presentation of Lion's Flag
Liao Ta-fu (Taiwan)	Twin Square Rods
Han Ch'ing-t'ang (Shantung)	Yang T'ai-chi
Fu Sung-nan	Shao-lin Long Boxing
Liu Mu-sen (Kiangsu)	Shao-lin Short Boxing
Ts'ai K'un-hsu (Taiwan)	The Hoofs of a White Horse
Wang Sung-t'ing (Shantung)	T'ai I Ch'uan
Liang T'ang-jung (Fukien)	Warrior Pa Wang Drawing His Bow
Ku Chung-nien	Seven Knot Soft Whip
Kao Sen-yao (Taiwan)	One Way Out
Liao Wu-ch'ang (Taiwan)	Monkey Boxing
Kao Sen-huang (Taiwan)	Five Tigers Down the Mountain
Ku Chung-nien and Liu Mu-sen	Shao-lin Close Fighting
Li Ch'ing-han (Kwangtung)	Lohan Boxing
Fu Chia-pin	Shao-lin Short Boxing
Liang T'ang-jung (Fukien)	Pa-kua Sword
Fu Chia-pin and Fu Sung-nan	Sword and Rod Countering the Spear
Han Ling-ling (Shantung)	K'un Wu Sword
Hung I-hsiang (Taiwan)	Hsing-i Ch'uan

Liao Wu-ch'ang (Taiwan)	Shield and Sword
Liu Mu-sen	Blue Steel Sword
Liao Ta-fu (Taiwan)	Hacker Attacking the Horse
Weng Yu-ch'uan (Hopeh) and Han Ch'ing-t'ang (Shantung)	T'ai-chi Pushing Hands
Wang Sung-t'ing (Shantung)	T'ai I Sword
Ku Chung-nien	Single Spring-Autumn Sword
Liu Mu-sen	Hacker
Li Ch'ing-han and Fu Sung-nan	Close Fighting of Pa Chi Ch'uan
Han Ch'ing-t'ang and Han Ling-ling (Shantung)	Swordplay
Fu Sung-nan	Single Sword
Liao Wu-ch'ang	Ch'in Ch'iung's Killing Square Rods
Wang Sung-t'ing (Shantung)	Eight Drunken Fairies
Liu Mu-sen	Plum Flower Spear
Fu Chia-pin and Fu Sung-nan	Hacker Countering Spear
Ts'ai K'un-hsu (Taiwan)	Drunken Boxing
Liang T'ang-jung (Fukien)	T'ai Tsu's Boxing While Swallowing a Bronze Ball
Liu Mu-sen and Li Ch'ing-han	Unarmed Defense Against the Sword
Kao Sen-yao and Kao Sen-huang (Taiwan)	Shao-lin Close Fighting
Wang Sung-t'ing	Mantis Boxing
Liao Wu-ch'ang, Hung I-hsiang, and Kao Sen-huang	Tile and Brick Breaking
Chang Wen-fu	Chinese Wrestling
P'an Tso-min	Thirteen Postures of Ch'en Chia Kou's T'ai-chi
Chang Hsing-i	Seven Knot Whip
Students of P'an Wen-tou	Police Techniques
Wu Han-chung	Eighteen Steps of Shao-lin Boxing
Li Tao-kuei	Killing the Tiger

I Te-k'un	Shao-lin Endless Boxing
Fu Chia-pin	Short Boxing
Liu Mu-sen	Short Boxing
Wu Chao-hsiang	Hsing-i Ch'uan of Shansi
Han Ch'ing-t'ang	T'ai Tsu Long Boxing
Yuan Tao (Anhwei)	Liang-i Sword
Lin Jih-sheng	Iron Bridge
Ch'en P'an-ling (Honan)	Synthetic Boxing
Su Ch'eng and Shen Ch'un-hui	Chinese Wrestling
Liu Pao-ch'uan and Hsiao I-hsien	Chinese Wrestling
Shang Tung-sheng (Hopeh)	Lohan Boxing
Wu Han-chung and Chang Hsing-i	Two Swords Defeating the Spear
P'an Wen-tou	Pa Chi Boxing
Hung I-hsiang (Taiwan)	New Boxing
Ch'en Chin-sheng and others	Police Techniques
Yuan Fa-tung	White Crane Boxing
Students of Wang Yen-nien	T'ai-chi Boxing
Chang Kai-yun	Shao-lin New Boxing
Wang Chin-ch'i	White Crane Boxing
Ch'en Chi	Violent Tiger Rushing From Woods
Ch'en I-ch'ou	T'ai Tsu Boxing
Kung Hsien-chou	Floating Legs
Kao Sen-huang	Shao-lin Chi-chi Boxing
Chang San-ching	Shao-lin Yung Ch'un Boxing
Ho Chao-sheng	Eight Steps of White Crane Boxing
Ch'eng Min-lin and Wang Shu-chun	Close Fighting of White Crane
Sang Tan-chi	Pi Boxing
Wang Shu-chin	Pa-kua and Hsing-i Boxing
Wang Yen-nien and Wang Jui-yuan	Close Fighting

Notes

Introduction

1. *Secrets of Shaolin Temple Boxing; Pa-kua: Chinese Boxing for Fitness and Self-defense;* and *Asian Fighting Arts.*

2. *Kung fu* can mean time spent or skill achieved at an endeavor. Traditionally, it has been used as a generic term for physical culture.

The Not-so-little Elephant

1. Krishnamurti, the contemporary Indian philosopher, is one of my teachers in the art of living, and it would not do to pass him by too quickly. Krishnamurti believes that a man is his own salvation and that Truth can only be experienced directly at the moment it happens. Any thought or intellectual projection of the Truth is a step away from it. Erich Fromm, in *The Art of Loving*, gets close by stating that a discipline should not be practiced like a rule imposed on oneself from the outside; rather it should become an expression of one's own will. It is felt as pleasant, and one slowly accustoms oneself to a kind of behavior that one would eventually miss if one stopped practicing it. While not holding with Krishnamurti that leaders and followers exploit each other, Fromm does feel that the most important requirement is the simple presence of a mature loving person. And that is what a teacher should be.

2. "*Ch'i* denotes the psychophysiological power associated with blood and breath," according to the scholar W. T. Chan. Most authorities simply translate it "intrinsic energy."

3. The core of this teaching may be seen in my *Pa-kua: Chinese Boxing for Fitness and Self-defense.*

The Monkey Boxer

1. I used some of the medicines for short periods only, never trusting them for long. They probably are better than I thought, having a long history of empirical testing behind them. In 1965 a mainland journal of traditional Chinese medicine carried an article on a bruise-resolving analgesic powder to treat injuries received from falls and beatings. Tested over several years, it purportedly regu-

lates the body energy and activates the blood. Among other herbs, it contains myrrh, frankincense, peach and almond seeds, white peony, and Szechwan aconite.

2. I am not convinced that this is pure deceit. Recent scientific work in the United States on biological rhythms indicates that man has many "clocks" or rhythms: pulse rate, blood production by the heart, the circulation of red and white blood cells, the amount of protein in the blood, the cir-culatory blood volume, blood pressure, and many others. Toxins injected in mice at 8 P.M. killed 80 percent of those injected, whereas only 20 percent of those injected at midnight died; lethality clearly depended on the time the mice were injected. Moreover, other tests showed that the creatures' strength varied with the time of day. Even though we know little of these internal processes, this work is sufficiently suggestive to preclude our discrediting the correlation of striking to time. (I might note in passing that my thinking on this point has changed since the publication of *Asian Fighting Arts*.)

3. He also arranged for several filming sessions. Because these demonstrations included so broad a spectrum of the boxing art, I list them at appendix E.

The Guerrilla General

1. Westerners have trouble squaring a religion like Buddhism with fighting. Certainly never in Christendom was there an institutionalized boxing like that at the Shao-lin temples. But the boxing done was for individual self-defense; Buddhism as a stimulus for collective war simply did not exist (would that Christianity, Islam, and others could make that claim!). Like Hinduism, its parent religion, Buddhism prohibits the killing of all beings. Unlike Hindu-ism's motivation (nonviolence), the Buddhist proscription springs from *metta*, or "loving kindness." A sincere Buddhist will not kill even in self-defense. He may injure an attacker, but even this is cause for regret. Karma is king here; extinction of desire is central. If an attacker is killed unintentionally, however, merit is not lost.

Master of the Five Excellences

1. The term is pronounced *tie-ji*, and the second character is different from the one romanized *ch'i* (and pronounced *chee*), which is discussed extensively throughout this book. For a fuller description, see my book, coauthored with Cheng Man-ch'ing, *T'ai-chi*.

2. The mind focuses on only this. And it must be controlled. A Buddhist meditation master once wrote: "Keeping the mind under control is like tether-ing a wild bull. He calms down after a while. Finally, he becomes so used to the tether that even if you release him he will not go away."

3. From *T'ai-chi Ch'uan Ching*.

4. Yang Lu-ch'an was active in the mid-nineteenth century. Pan-hou and Chien-hou died in 1881 and 1917, respectively.

5. The cultivation of the ch'i is important in the disciplines of painting and calligraphy. In the latter, instead of the short, hard-bristled brush wielded by a hand resting wrist on table, master calligraphers keep their wrists and elbows devoid of any support and perform their artistry using long, soft-bristled brushes held on a line with their noses. This is tiring, and, as one once told me, it is a physical education in itself.

6. Harsh he may have been, but his technique was superb. His trigger-force, concentrated energy was such that he was never defeated. Cheng once saw him extinguish a candle from six feet away by gesturing with his hand, a feat be-speaking tremendous ch'i.

7. Yang's ability did not stop with T'ai-chi. He also had superlative skill with the sword. In Nanking he once faced Li Ching-lin, one of China's top swords-men, and knocked Li's sword out of his hand right after they squared off.

8. The three stages of T'ai-chi skill are as follows:

I. MAN: the ch'i circulates.
   A. Ch'i goes from shoulder to fingers.
   B. Ch'i goes from thigh to the sole of the foot.
   C. Ch'i goes from vertebrae to the top of the head.
II. EARTH: the ch'i penetrates the bones.
   A. Ch'i goes to the *tan t'ien*. ·
   B. Ch'i focuses on the sole.
   C. Ch'i permeates the entire body.
III. HEAVEN: interpreting the energy.
   A. "Hear" energy.
   B. Understand energy (unconscious receiving).
   C. The summit.

9. The Taoist Ch'ang-ch'un once visited Genghis Khan and advised him to sleep alone for one month. The Ancients said: "To take medicine for a thou-

sand days does less good than to lie alone for a single night."

The Wrestling Champion
1. For more on shuai chiao, see *Asian Fighting Arts.*

Other Teachers
1. Currently Kuo is teaching boxing in San Francisco.

Teachers in Southern Taiwan
1. I heard several stories on the origin of White Crane Boxing. In the most romantic one, a boxing teacher offered his beautiful daughter to anyone who could best him. A student of poor character took him up on it and killed him. The bereaved girl agreed to marry the man but only after a three-year period of mourning. She used this time to practice boxing but still fell short of her antagonist's ability, until, one day, she saw a crane, watched it, fascinated by its power, and created the method with which she revenged her father.
2. See *Secrets of Shaolin Temple Boxing* for my version of this book. After meeting Wang, I learned that the book, while fairly unknown on Taiwan, had had a wide readership among boxers on the mainland. Historian Chou Ch'i-ch'un told me that the book had been castrated by Ch'en T'ieh-sheng, a Cantonese journalist. In my treatment, I attempted to rid the book of distortions and put it back in its original form.

Afterword
1. This idea is beautifully illustrated in the short story by Nakashima Ton entitled *The Expert* (*Encounter*, May, 1958). If the physical were all or even primary, we would not be too far removed from Chu P'ing-man, who, Chuang Tzu wrote, spent a thousand in gold and three years learning dragon killing from Hunchback Yi only to find there was no place for him to practice his art.

Appendix A
1. Because I lack some of the cited titles in Chinese, they are given here in English. See bibliography for all the information available at the present time.

Glossary

Aikido, 合気道, Meeting Spirit Way, a Japanese martial art
atemi, 当身, the art of attacking vital points

Bo-jutsu, 棒術, Stick Fighting, a Japanese martial art

che-tieh, 摺叠, folding
ch'i, 気, vital energy
ch'i kung, 気工, cultivating the ch'i
chin chung chao, 金鐘罩, gold bell cover, a protective technique of Chinese boxing
ching, 精, an essence formed in the kidneys
ching, 静, static posture (ch'i-kung)
ching, 勁, tenacious energy
chin-na, 擒拿, the art of seizing
ch'i-yun, 気運, ch'i in movement
ch'uan fa, 拳法, Chinese boxing
ch'uan shu, 拳術, Chinese boxing

dan, 段, grade, rank
dōjō, 道場, drill hall

goshin-jutsu, 護身術, the art of self-defense
gyaku-te, 逆手, the art of bone locking

hadaka-jime, 裸締, naked strangle (judo)
haraigoshi, 払腰, sweeping loins throw (judo)
heng-ch'uan, 横拳, crossing, one of the five forms in Hsing-i Boxing
Hsing-i, 形意, the Form of Mind, one of the three internal boxing systems
hu k'ou, 虎口, tiger mouth: space between the stretched thumb and index finger

i, 意, mind, intent

jen, 燕, a vital point
jūdōgi, 柔道着, judo practice suit

kata, 形, a form
kiai, 気合, spirit shout
Kiaijutsu, 気合術, the Art of the Spirit Shout, a Japanese martial art
Kou Ch'uan, 狗拳, Dog Boxing
kung chia, 功架, the basic postures of T'ai-chi Boxing
kung fu, 功夫, skill, time, ability

li, 力, forceful strength
liang-i, 両儀, two powers of yin and yang, a type of Chinese boxing

makiwara, 卷藁, a hitting post

nei-chia, 内家, the internal systems of Chinese boxing
nidan, 二段, second grade

ouchigari, 大内刈, big inner reaping throw (judo)

Pai-hao Ch'uan, 白鶴拳, or Hao Ch'uan, 鶴拳, White Crane Boxing
Pa-kua, 八卦, Eight Diagrams, one of the three internal boxing systems
pa tuan chin, Chinese calisthenics
p'eng, 掤, a basic T'ai-chi posture
peng ch'uan, 崩拳, crushing, one of the five forms of Hsing-i Boxing
p'i ch'uan, 劈拳, splitting, one of the five forms of Hsing-i Boxing
p'i mao, 皮毛, skin (and) hair, i.e., superficial

sandan, 三段, third grade
Shao-lin Mei-hua Ch'uan, 少林梅花拳, Shao-lin Plum Blossom Boxing
shih-san shih, 十三勢, the thirteen operations of T'ai-chi
shime, 締, strangling
shuai chiao, 摔跤, Chinese wrestling

Ta-ch'eng Ch'uan, 大成拳, Great Achievement Boxing

Ta Hsing Ch'uan, 大猩拳, Monkey Boxing

T'ai-chi Ch'uan, 太極拳, Grand Ultimate Boxing

t'ai-i, 太乙, the great entity, a sword form

tai-otoshi, 体落, body drop throw (judo)

ta-lu, 大攄, the cornering steps of T'ai-chi

tan-t'ien, 丹田, sea of ch'i, the psychic center just below the navel

tien-ch'i, 恬気, inspired ch'i

tien-hsueh, 点穴, the art of attacking vital points

t'i fang, 提放, lift-let go, a T'ai-chi technique

tu, 兔, a vital point

t'ui shou, 推手, pushing hands, a stage of T'ai-chi Boxing

tung, 動, moving postures of ch'i-kung

uchimata, 内股, inner thigh throw (judo)

ukemi, 受身, ways of falling (judo)

Wu, 武, a main style of T'ai-chi

wu-shu, 武術, Chinese martial arts

Wutang, 武当, an ancient school of Inner Boxing

yang, 陽, male principle, active

Yang, 楊, one of four schools of T'ai-chi

yin, 陰, female principle, passive

Yunnan Lien Pu Ch'uan, 雲南連歩拳, Consecutive Step Yunnan Boxing.

Bibliography

Brunner, Constantin. *Science, Spirit, Superstition.* London: George Allen and Unwin Ltd., 1968.

Buytendijk, F. J. *Pain.* Westport, Conn.: Greenwood Press, Inc., 1973.

Cheng Man-ch'ing. *Cheng-tzu T'ai-chi Ch'uan Shih-san P'ien* (Cheng's Thirteen Chapters on T'ai-chi Boxing). Taipei: published privately, 1960.

Cheng Man-ch'ing, and Smith, Robert W. *T'ai-chi.* Rutland, Vt.: Charles E. Tuttle Co., 1967.

Ch'en Yen-ling. *T'ai-chi Ch'uan Tao Chien Kan San-shou Ho-pien* (T'ai-chi Boxing, with Broadsword, Sword, Stick, and Free Hand Techniques). Hong Kong: published privately, 1943.

Chiao Kuo-shui. *Ch'i-kung Yang-sheng-fa* (A Method of Nourishing Health). Shanghai: Shanghai Scientific Techniques Press, 1964.

Chin I-ming. *Wu-tang Ch'uan-shu Mi Chueh* (Secrets of Wutang Boxing). n.p.: 1928.

Draeger, Donn F., and Smith, Robert W. *Asian Fighting Arts.* Tokyo: Kodansha International Ltd., 1969.

Fokine, Michel. *Memoirs of a Ballet Master.* Boston: Little, Brown & Co., 1961.

Han Ch'ing-t'ang. *Ching-ch'a Ying-yung Chi-neng* (Techniques for Police Use). Taipei: published privately, 1958.

Harrison, E. J. *The Fighting Spirit of Japan.* New York: Sterling Publishing Co., Inc., n.d.

Hsu Chen. *T'ai-chi Ch'uan K'ao Hsin Lu* (Investigation of the True History of T'ai-chi Boxing). Nanking: 1937; reprinted Taipei: 1967.

—*T'ai-chi Ch'uan Pien Wei* (Distinguishing the False from the True in T'ai-chi Boxing). n.p., n.d.

Hsu Lung-hou. *T'ai-chi Ch'uan Shih T'u Chieh* (Illustrated Explanation of T'ai-chi Boxing). n.p., n.d.

140

Li I-yu. *T'ai-chi Ch'uan Hsiao Hsu* (Brief Preface to T'ai-chi Boxing). n.p., n.d.

Seldes, Gilbert. *The Seven Lively Arts*. Cranbury, N. J.: A. S. Barnes & Co., Inc., 1962.

Smith, Robert W. *Pa-kua: Chinese Boxing for Fitness and Self-defense*. Tokyo: Kodansha International Ltd., 1967.

Smith, Robert W. *Secrets of Shaolin Temple Boxing*. Rutland, Vt.: Charles E. Tuttle Co., 1964.

Sung Yuan-ch'iao. *Sung T'ai-chi Kung Yuan Liu Chi Chih-p'ai Kao* (Sung's T'ai-chi and Its Offshoots). n.p., n.d.

Sze Mai-mai. *The Way of Chinese Painting*. New York: Random House, Inc., n.d.

T'ai-chi Ch'uan Ching (T'ai-chi Boxing Classics). n.p., n.d.

T'ang Hao. *Ch'en T'ai-chi Ch'uan* (Ch'en's T'ai-chi Boxing). n. p., n.d.

von Durckheim, Karlfried. *Hara: The Vital Center of Man*. London: George Allen and Unwin Ltd., 1962.

Wan Lai-sheng. *Wu-shu Nei-wai-kung*. (The Internal and External Fighting. Arts). Shanghai: 1926; reprinted Taipei: 1962.

Wang Chung-yueh. *T'ai-chi Ch'uan Lun* (Theory of T'ai-chi Boxing). n.p., n.d.

Wang Hsin-wu. *T'ai-chi Ch'uan Fa Ch'an Tsung* (Orthodox T'ai-chi Boxing). n.p., n.d.

Wu, K. C. *The Lane of Eternal Stability*. New York: Crown Publishers, Inc., 1962.

Index

Conventions:

Wade-Giles spelling of original is followed. Chinese family names are in bold-italic, and book titles are in light italic.

Names with intervening apostrophes appear before names identically lettered, but without apostrophes: in some cases, typesetting errors in the original may produce the same name in more than one form.

Boxing styles and attributes appear all-minuscule, except where a family name is used—eg, Yang style t'ai-chi.

The book's Appendix E is not indexed.

The author of this index, Paul Kunino Lynch of Sydney, claims moral right to this work and yields copyright.

Users are requested to reproduce only with attribution to Paul Kunino Lynch; otherwise, there is no restriction on reproduction.